A Prentice Hall Pocket Reader

• •

LITERATURE

Edited by

Mary McAleer Balkun

Seton Hall University

PEARSON

Prentice
Hall

Upper Saddle River, New Jersey 07458

© 2005 by PEARSON EDUCATION, INC.
Upper Saddle River, New Jersey 07458

10 9 8 7 6 5 4 3 2 1

ISBN 0-13-189558-3

Printed in the United States of America

CONTENTS

1

SHORT STORIES

A ROSE FOR EMILY

William Faulkner

I

When Miss Emily Grierson died, our whole town went to her 1
funeral: the men through a sort of respectful affection for a fallen
monument, the women mostly out of curiosity to see the inside of her
house, which no one save an old manservant—a combined gardener
and cook—had seen in at least ten years.

It was a big, squarish frame house that had once been white, dec- 2
orated with cupolas and spires and scrolled balconies in the heavily
lightsome style of the seventies, set on what had once been our most
select street. But garages and cotton gins had encroached and oblit-
erated even the august names of that neighborhood; only Miss
Emily's house was left, lifting its stubborn and coquettish decay
above the cotton wagons and the gasoline pumps—an eyesore
among eyesores. And now Miss Emily had gone to join the represen-
tatives of those august names where they lay in the cedar-bemused
cemetery among the ranked and anonymous graves of Union and
Confederate soldiers who fell at the battle of Jefferson.

Alive, Miss Emily had been a tradition, a duty, and a care; a sort 3
of hereditary obligation upon the town, dating from that day in 1894
when Colonel Sartoris, the mayor—he who fathered the edict that no
Negro woman should appear on the streets without an apron—
remitted her taxes, the dispensation dating from the death of her
father on into perpetuity. Not that Miss Emily would have accepted
charity. Colonel Sartoris invented an involved tale to the effect that

Miss Emily's father had loaned money to the town, which the town, as a matter of business, preferred this way of repaying. Only a man of Colonel Sartoris' generation and thought could have invented it, and only a woman could have believed it.

When the next generation, with its more modern ideas, became 4 mayors and aldermen, this arrangement created some little dissatisfaction. On the first of the year they mailed her a tax notice. February came, and there was no reply. They wrote her a formal letter, asking her to call at the sheriff's office at her convenience. A week later the mayor wrote her himself, offering to call or to send his car for her, and received in reply a note on paper of an archaic shape, in a thin, flowing calligraphy in faded ink, to the effect that she no longer went out at all. The tax notice was also enclosed, without comment.

They called a special meeting of the Board of Aldermen. A depu- 5 tation waited upon her, knocked at the door through which no visitor had passed since she ceased giving china-painting lessons eight or ten years earlier. They were admitted by the old Negro into a dim hall from which a stairway mounted into still more shadow. It smelled of dust and disuse—a close, dank smell. The Negro led them into the parlor. It was furnished in heavy, leather-covered furniture. When the Negro opened the blinds of one window, they could see that the leather was cracked; and when they sat down, a faint dust rose sluggishly about their thighs, spinning with slow motes in the single sun-ray. On a tarnished gilt easel before the fireplace stood a crayon portrait of Miss Emily's father.

They rose when she entered—a small, fat woman in black, with 6 a thin gold chain descending to her waist and vanishing into her belt, leaning on an ebony cane with a tarnished gold head. Her skeleton was small and spare; perhaps that was why what would have been merely plumpness in another was obesity in her. She looked bloated, like a body long submerged in motionless water, and of that pallid hue. Her eyes, lost in the fatty ridges of her face, looked like two small pieces of coal pressed into a lump of dough as they moved from one face to another while the visitors stated their errand.

She did not ask them to sit. She just stood in the door and listened 7 quietly until the spokesman came to a stumbling halt. Then they could hear the invisible watch ticking at the end of the gold chain.

Her voice was dry and cold. "I have no taxes in Jefferson. Colonel Sartoris explained it to me. Perhaps one of you can gain access to the 8 city records and satisfy yourselves."

"But we have. We are the city authorities, Miss Emily. Didn't you 9 get a notice from the sheriff, signed by him?"

"I received a paper, yes," Miss Emily said. "Perhaps he considers 10
himself the sheriff . . . I have no taxes in Jefferson."
    "But there is nothing on the books to show that, you see. We 11
must go by the—"
    "See Colonel Sartoris. I have no taxes in Jefferson."   12
    "But, Miss Emily—"   13
    "See Colonel Sartoris." (Colonel Sartoris had been dead almost 14
ten years.) "I have no taxes in Jefferson. Tobe!" The Negro appeared.
"Show these gentlemen out."

II

    So she vanquished them, horse and foot, just as she had van- 15
quished their fathers thirty years before about the smell. That was
two years after her father's death and a short time after her sweetheart—the one we believed would marry her—had deserted her.
After her father's death she went out very little; after her sweetheart
went away, people hardly saw her at all. A few of the ladies had the
temerity to call, but were not received, and the only sign of life about
the place was the Negro man—a young man then—going in and out
with a market basket.
    "Just as if a man—any man—could keep a kitchen properly," the 16
ladies said; so they were not surprised when the smell developed. It
was another link between the gross, teeming world and the high and
mighty Griersons.
    A neighbor, a woman, complained to the mayor, Judge Stevens, 17
eighty years old.
    "But what will you have me do about it, madam?" he said.   18
    "Why, send her word to stop it," the woman said. "Isn't there a 19
law?"
    "I'm sure that won't be necessary," Judge Stevens said. "It's 20
probably just a snake or a rat that nigger of hers killed in the yard. I'll
speak to him about it."
    The next day he received two more complaints, one from a man 21
who came in diffident deprecation. "We really must do something
about it, Judge. I'd be the last one in the world to bother Miss Emily,
but we've got to do something." That night the Board of Aldermen
met—three graybeards and one younger man, a member of the rising
generation.
    "It's simple enough," he said. "Send her word to have her place 22
cleaned up. Give her a certain time to do it in, and if she don't . . ."

"Dammit, sir," Judge Stevens said, "will you accuse a lady to her 23 face of smelling bad?"

So the next night, after midnight, four men crossed Miss Emily's 24 lawn and slunk about the house like burglars, sniffing along the base of the brickwork and at the cellar openings while one of them performed a regular sowing motion with his hand out of a sack slung from his shoulder. They broke open the cellar door and sprinkled lime there, and in all the outbuildings. As they recrossed the lawn, a window that had been dark was lighted and Miss Emily sat in it, the light behind her, and her upright torso motionless as that of an idol. They crept quietly across the lawn and into the shadow of the locusts that lined the street. After a week or two the smell went away.

That was when people had begun to feel really sorry for her. 25 People in our town, remembering how old lady Wyatt, her great-aunt, had gone completely crazy at last, believed that the Griersons held themselves a little too high for what they really were. None of the young men were quite good enough for Miss Emily and such. We had long thought of them as a tableau, Miss Emily a slender figure in white in the background, her father a spraddled silhouette in the foreground, his back to her and clutching a horsewhip, the two of them framed by the back-flung front door. So when she got to be thirty and was still single, we were not pleased exactly, but vindicated; even with insanity in the family she wouldn't have turned down all of her chances if they had really materialized.

When her father died, it got about that the house was all that was 26 left to her; and in a way, people were glad. At last they could pity Miss Emily. Being left alone, and a pauper, she had become humanized. Now she too would know the old thrill and the old despair of a penny more or less.

The day after his death all the ladies prepared to call at the house 27 and offer condolence and aid, as is our custom. Miss Emily met them at the door, dressed as usual and with no trace of grief on her face. She told them that her father was not dead. She did that for three days, with the ministers calling on her, and the doctors, trying to persuade her to let them dispose of the body. Just as they were about to resort to law and force, she broke down, and they buried her father quickly.

We did not say she was crazy then. We believed she had to do 28 that. We remembered all the young men her father had driven away, and we knew that with nothing left, she would have to cling to that which had robbed her, as people will.

III

She was sick for a long time. When we saw her again, her hair 29 was cut short, making her look like a girl, with a vague resemblance to those angels in colored church windows—sort of tragic and serene.

The town had just let the contracts for paving the sidewalks, and 30 in the summer after her father's death they began the work. The construction company came with niggers and mules and machinery, and a foreman named Homer Barron, a Yankee—a big, dark, ready man, with a big voice and eyes lighter than his face. The little boys would follow in groups to hear him cuss the niggers, and the niggers singing in time to the rise and fall of picks. Pretty soon he knew everybody in town. Whenever you heard a lot of laughing anywhere about the square, Homer Barron would be in the center of the group. Presently we began to see him and Miss Emily on Sunday afternoons driving in the yellow-wheeled buggy and the matched team of bays from the livery stable.

At first we were glad that Miss Emily would have an interest, 31 because the ladies all said, "Of course a Grierson would not think seriously of a Northerner, a day laborer." But there were still others, older people, who said that even grief could not cause a real lady to forget *noblesse oblige*—without calling it *noblesse oblige*. They just said, "Poor Emily. Her kinsfolk should come to her." She had some kin in Alabama; but years ago her father had fallen out with them over the estate of old lady Wyatt, the crazy woman, and there was no communication between the two families. They had not even been represented at the funeral.

And as soon as the old people said, "Poor Emily," the whisper- 32 ing began. "Do you suppose it's really so?" they said to one another. "Of course it is. What else could. . . ." This behind their hands; rustling of craned silk and satin behind jalousies closed upon the sun of Sunday afternoon as the thin, swift clop-clop-clop of the matched team passed: "Poor Emily."

She carried her head high enough—even when we believed that 33 she was fallen. It was as if she demanded more than ever the recognition of her dignity as the last Grierson; as if it had wanted that touch of earthiness to reaffirm her imperviousness. Like when she bought the rat poison, the arsenic. That was over a year after they had begun to say "Poor Emily," and while the two female cousins were visiting her.

"I want some poison," she said to the druggist. She was over 34
thirty then, still a slight woman, though thinner than usual, with
cold, haughty black eyes in a face the flesh of which was strained
across the temples and about the eyesockets as you imagine a light-
house-keeper's face ought to look. "I want some poison," she said.
"Yes, Miss Emily. What kind? For rats and such? I'd recom—" 35
"I want the best you have. I don't care what kind." 36
The druggist named several. "They'll kill anything up to an ele- 37
phant. But what you want is—"
"Arsenic," Miss Emily said. "Is that a good one?" 38
"Is . . . arsenic? Yes, ma'am. But what you want—" 39
"I want arsenic." 40
The druggist looked down at her. She looked back at him, erect, 41
her face like a strained flag. "Why, of course," the druggist said. "If
that's what you want. But the law requires you to tell what you are
going to use it for."

Miss Emily just stared at him, her head tilted back in order to 42
look him eye for eye, until he looked away and went and got the
arsenic and wrapped it up. The Negro delivery boy brought her the
package; the druggist didn't come back. When she opened the package at home there was written on the box, under the skull and bones:
"For rats."

IV

So the next day we all said, "She will kill herself"; and we said it 43
would be the best thing. When she had first begun to be seen with
Homer Barron, we had said, "She will marry him." Then we said,
"She will persuade him yet," because Homer himself had
remarked—he liked men, and it was known that he drank with the
younger men in the Elks' Club—that he was not a marrying man.
Later we said, "Poor Emily" behind the jalousies as they passed on
Sunday afternoon in the glittering buggy, Miss Emily with her head
high and Homer Barron with his hat cocked and a cigar in his teeth,
reins and whip in a yellow glove.

Then some of the ladies began to say that it was a disgrace to the 44
town and a bad example to the young people. The men did not want
to interfere, but at last the ladies forced the Baptist minister—Miss
Emily's people were Episcopal—to call upon her. He would never
divulge what happened during that interview, but he refused to go
back again. The next Sunday they again drove about the streets, and

the following day the minister's wife wrote to Miss Emily's relations in Alabama.

So she had blood-kin under her roof again and we sat back to 45 watch developments. At first nothing happened. Then we were sure that they were to be married. We learned that Miss Emily had been to the jeweler's and ordered a man's toilet set in silver, with the letters H. B. on each piece. Two days later we learned that she had bought a complete outfit of men's clothing, including a nightshirt, and we said, "They are married." We were really glad. We were glad because the two female cousins were even more Grierson than Miss Emily had ever been.

So we were not surprised when Homer Barron—the streets had 46 been finished some time since—was gone. We were a little disappointed that there was not a public blowing-off, but we believed that he had gone on to prepare for Miss Emily's coming, or to give her a chance to get rid of the cousins. (By that time it was a cabal, and we were all Miss Emily's allies to help circumvent the cousins.) Sure enough, after another week they departed. And, as we had expected all along, within three days Homer Barron was back in town. A neighbor saw the Negro man admit him at the kitchen door at dusk one evening.

And that was the last we saw of Homer Barron. And of Miss 47 Emily for some time. The Negro man went in and out with the market basket, but the front door remained closed. Now and then we would see her at a window for a moment, as the men did that night when they sprinkled the lime, but for almost six months she did not appear on the streets. Then we knew that this was to be expected too; as if that quality of her father which had thwarted her woman's life so many times had been too virulent and too furious to die.

When we next saw Miss Emily, she had grown fat and her hair 48 was turning gray. During the next few years it grew grayer and grayer until it attained an even pepper-and-salt iron-gray, when it ceased turning. Up to the day of her death at seventy-four it was still that vigorous iron-gray, like the hair of an active man.

From that time on her front door remained closed, save for a 49 period of six or seven years, when she was about forty, during which she gave lessons in china-painting. She fitted up a studio in one of the downstairs rooms, where the daughters and granddaughters of Colonel Sartoris' contemporaries were sent to her with the same regularity and in the same spirit that they were sent to church on Sundays with a twenty-five-cent piece for the collection plate. Meanwhile her taxes had been remitted.

Then the newer generation became the backbone and the spirit 50
of the town, and the painting pupils grew up and fell away and did
not send their children to her with boxes of color and tedious brushes
and pictures cut from the ladies' magazines. The front door closed
upon the last one and remained closed for good. When the town got
free postal delivery, Miss Emily alone refused to let them fasten the
metal numbers above her door and attach a mailbox to it. She would
not listen to them.

Daily, monthly, yearly we watched the Negro grow grayer and 51
more stooped, going in and out with the market basket. Each
December we sent her a tax notice, which would be returned by the
post office a week later, unclaimed. Now and then we would see her
in one of the downstairs windows—she had evidently shut up the
top floor of the house—like the carven torso of an idol in a niche,
looking or not looking at us, we could never tell which. Thus she
passed from generation to generation—dear, inescapable, impervi-
ous, tranquil, and perverse.

And so she died. Fell ill in the house filled with dust and shad- 52
ows, with only a doddering Negro man to wait on her. We did not
even know she was sick; we had long since given up trying to get any
information from the Negro. He talked to no one, probably not even
to her, for his voice had grown harsh and rusty, as if from disuse.

She died in one of the downstairs rooms, in a heavy walnut bed 53
with a curtain, her gray head propped on a pillow yellow and moldy
with age and lack of sunlight.

V

The Negro met the first of the ladies at the front door and let 54
them in, with their hushed, sibilant voices and their quick, curious
glances, and then he disappeared. He walked right through the
house and out the back and was not seen again.

The two female cousins came at once. They held the funeral on 55
the second day, with the town coming to look at Miss Emily beneath
a mass of bought flowers, with the crayon face of her father musing
profoundly above the bier and the ladies sibilant and macabre; and
the very old men—some in their brushed Confederate uniforms—on
the porch and the lawn, talking of Miss Emily as if she had been a
contemporary of theirs, believing that they had danced with her and
courted her perhaps, confusing time with its mathematical progres-
sion, as the old do, to whom all the past is not a diminishing road but,

instead, a huge meadow which no winter ever quite touches, divided from them now by the narrow bottle-neck of the most recent decade of years.

Already we knew that there was one room in that region above 56 stairs which no one had seen in forty years, and which would have to be forced. They waited until Miss Emily was decently in the ground before they opened it.

The violence of breaking down the door seemed to fill this room 57 with pervading dust. A thin, acrid pall as of the tomb seemed to lie everywhere upon this room decked and furnished as for a bridal: upon the valance curtains of faded rose color, upon the rose-shaded lights, upon the dressing table, upon the delicate array of crystal and the man's toilet things backed with tarnished silver, silver so tarnished that the monogram was obscured. Among them lay a collar and tie, as if they had just been removed, which, lifted, left upon the surface a pale crescent in the dust. Upon a chair hung the suit, carefully folded; beneath it the two mute shoes and the discarded socks.

The man himself lay in the bed. 58

For a long while we just stood there, looking down at the pro- 59 found and fleshless grin. The body had apparently once lain in the attitude of an embrace, but now the long sleep that outlasts love, that conquers even the grimace of love, had cuckolded him. What was left of him, rotted beneath what was left of the nightshirt, had become inextricable from the bed in which he lay; and upon him and upon the pillow beside him lay that even coating of the patient and biding dust.

Then we noticed that in the second pillow was the indentation of 60 a head. One of us lifted something from it, and leaning forward, that faint and invisible dust dry and acrid in the nostrils, we saw a long strand of iron-gray hair.

THE LOTTERY

Shirley Jackson

The morning of June 27th was clear and sunny, with the fresh 1
warmth of a full summer day; the flowers were blossoming profusely
and the grass was richly green. The people of the village began to
gather in the square, between the post office and the bank, around
ten o'clock; in some towns there were so many people that the lottery
took two days and had to be started on June 26th, but in this village,
where there were only about three hundred people, the whole lottery
took less than two hours, so it could begin at ten o'clock in the morning and still be through in time to allow the villagers to get home for
noon dinner.

The children assembled first, of course. School was recently over 2
for the summer, and the feeling of liberty sat uneasily on most of
them; they tended to gather together quietly for a while before they
broke into boisterous play, and their talk was still of the classroom
and the teacher, of books and reprimands. Bobby Martin had already
stuffed his pockets full of stones, and the other boys soon followed
his example, selecting the smoothest and roundest stones; Bobby and
Harry Jones and Dickie Delacroix—the villagers pronounced this
name "Dellacroy"—eventually made a great pile of stones in one corner of the square and guarded it against the raids of the other boys.
The girls stood aside, talking among themselves, looking over their
shoulders at the boys, and the very small children rolled in the dust
or clung to the hands of their older brothers or sisters.

Soon the men began to gather, surveying their own children, 3
speaking of planting and rain, tractors and taxes. They stood
together, away from the pile of stones in the corner, and their jokes
were quiet and they smiled rather than laughed. The women, wearing faded house dresses and sweaters, came shortly after their men-
folk. They greeted one another and exchanged bits of gossip as they
went to join their husbands. Soon the women, standing by their husbands, began to call to their children, and the children came reluc-
tantly, having to be called four or five times. Bobby Martin ducked
under his mother's grasping hand and ran, laughing, back to the pile
of stones. His father spoke up sharply, and Bobby came quickly and
took his place between his father and his oldest brother.

The lottery was conducted—as were the square dances, the teen- 4
age club, the Halloween program—by Mr. Summers, who had time
and energy to devote to civic activities. He was a round-faced, jovial
man and he ran the coal business, and people were sorry for him,
because he had no children and his wife was a scold. When he
arrived in the square, carrying the black wooden box, there was a
murmur of conversation among the villagers, and he waved and
called, "Little late today, folks." The postmaster, Mr. Graves, followed
him, carrying a three-legged stool, and the stool was put in the center of the square and Mr. Summers set the black box down on it. The
villagers kept their distance, leaving a space between themselves and
the stool, and when Mr. Summers said, "Some of you fellows want to
give me a hand?" there was a hesitation before two men, Mr. Martin
and his oldest son, Baxter, came forward to hold the box steady on
the stool while Mr. Summers stirred up the papers inside it.

The original paraphernalia for the lottery had been lost long ago, 5
and the black box now resting on the stool had been put into use even
before Old Man Warner, the oldest man in town, was born. Mr.
Summers spoke frequently to the villagers about making a new box,
but no one liked to upset even as much tradition as was represented
by the black box. There was a story that the present box had been
made with some pieces of the box that had preceded it, the one that
had been constructed when the first people settled down to make a
village here. Every year, after the lottery, Mr. Summers began talking
again about a new box, but every year the subject was allowed to
fade off without anything's being done. The black box grew shabbier
each year; by now it was no longer completely black but splintered
badly along one side to show the original wood color, and in some
places faded or stained.

Mr. Martin and his oldest son, Baxter, held the black box securely 6
on the stool until Mr. Summers had stirred the papers thoroughly
with his hand. Because so much of the ritual had been forgotten or
discarded, Mr. Summers had been successful in having slips of paper
substituted for the chips of wood that had been used for generations.
Chips of wood, Mr. Summers had argued, had been all very well
when the village was tiny, but now that the population was more
than three hundred and likely to keep on growing, it was necessary
to use something that would fit more easily into the black box. The
night before the lottery, Mr. Summers and Mr. Graves made up the
slips of paper and put them in the box, and it was then taken to the

safe of Mr. Summers' coal company and locked up until Mr. Summers was ready to take it to the square next morning. The rest of the year, the box was put away, sometimes one place, sometimes another; it had spent one year in Mr. Graves's barn and another year underfoot in the post office, and sometimes it was set on a shelf in the Martin grocery and left there.

There was a great deal of fussing to be done before Mr. Summers 7 declared the lottery open. There were the lists to make up—of heads of families, heads of households in each family, members of each household in each family. There was the proper swearing-in of Mr. Summers by the postmaster, as the official of the lottery; at one time, some people remembered, there had been a recital of some sort, performed by the official of the lottery, a perfunctory, tuneless chant that had been rattled off duly each year; some people believed that the official of the lottery used to stand just so when he said or sang it, others believed that he was supposed to walk among the people, but years and years ago this part of the ritual had been allowed to lapse. There had been, also, a ritual salute, which the official of the lottery had had to use in addressing each person who came up to draw from the box, but this also had changed with time, until now it was felt necessary only for the official to speak to each person approaching. Mr. Summers was very good at all this; in his clean white shirt and blue jeans, with one hand resting carelessly on the black box, he seemed very proper and important as he talked interminably to Mr. Graves and the Martins.

Just as Mr. Summers finally left off talking and turned to the 8 assembled villagers, Mrs. Hutchinson came hurriedly along the path to the square, her sweater thrown over her shoulders, and slid into place in the back of the crowd. "Clean forgot what day it was," she said to Mrs. Delacroix, who stood next to her, and they both laughed softly. "Thought my old man was out back stacking wood," Mrs. Hutchinson went on, "and then I looked out the window and the kids was gone, and then I remembered it was the twenty-seventh and came a-running." She dried her hands on her apron, and Mrs. Delacroix said, "You're in time, though. They're still talking away up there."

Mrs. Hutchinson craned her neck to see through the crowd and 9 found her husband and children standing near the front. She tapped Mrs. Delacroix on the arm as a farewell and began to make her way through the crowd. The people separated good-humoredly to let her through; two or three people said, in voices just loud enough to be heard across the crowd, "Here comes your Missus, Hutchinson," and

"Bill, she made it after all." Mrs. Hutchinson reached her husband, and Mr. Summers, who had been waiting, said cheerfully, "Thought we were going to have to get on without you, Tessie." Mrs. Hutchinson said, grinning, "Wouldn't have me leave m'dishes in the sink, now, would you, Joe?," and soft laughter ran through the crowd as the people stirred back into position after Mrs. Hutchinson's arrival.

"Well, now," Mr. Summers said soberly, "guess we better get   10 started, get this over with, so's we can go back to work. Anybody ain't here?"

"Dunbar," several people said. "Dunbar, Dunbar."   11

Mr. Summers consulted his list. "Clyde Dunbar," he said. "That's   12 right. He's broke his leg, hasn't he? Who's drawing for him?"

"Me, I guess," a woman said, and Mr. Summers turned to look at   13 her. "Wife draws for her husband," Mr. Summers said. "Don't you have a grown boy to do it for you, Janey?" Although Mr. Summers and everyone else in the village knew the answer perfectly well, it was the business of the official of the lottery to ask such questions formally. Mr. Summers waited with an expression of polite interest while Mrs. Dunbar answered.

"Horace's not but sixteen yet," Mrs. Dunbar said regretfully.   14 "Guess I gotta fill in for the old man this year."

"Right," Mr. Summers said. He made a note on the list he was   15 holding. Then he asked, "Watson boy drawing this year?"

A tall boy in the crowd raised his hand. "Here," he said. "I'm   16 drawing for m'mother and me." He blinked his eyes nervously and ducked his head as several voices in the crowd said things like "Good fellow, Jack," and "Glad to see your mother's got a man to do it."

"Well," Mr. Summers said, "guess that's everyone. Old Man   17 Warner make it?"

"Here," a voice said, and Mr. Summers nodded.   18

A sudden hush fell on the crowd as Mr. Summers cleared his   19 throat and looked at the list. "All ready?" he called. "Now, I'll read the names—heads of families first—and the men come up and take a paper out of the box. Keep the paper folded in your hand without looking at it until everyone has had a turn. Everything clear?"

The people had done it so many times that they only half listened   20 to the directions; most of them were quiet, wetting their lips, not looking around. Then Mr. Summers raised one hand high and said, "Adams." A man disengaged himself from the crowd and came forward. "Hi, Steve," Mr. Summers said, and Mr. Adams said, "Hi, Joe."

They grinned at one another humorlessly and nervously. Then Mr. Adams reached into the black box and took out a folded paper. He held it firmly by one corner as he turned and went hastily back to his place in the crowd, where he stood a little apart from his family, not looking down at his hand.

"Allen," Mr. Summers said. "Anderson. . . . Bentham."   21

"Seems like there's no time at all between lotteries any more,"   22
Mrs. Delacroix said to Mrs. Graves in the back row. "Seems like we got through with the last one only last week."

"Time sure goes fast," Mrs. Graves said.   23

"Clark. . . . Delacroix."   24

"There goes my old man," Mrs. Delacroix said. She held her   25
breath while her husband went forward.

"Dunbar," Mr. Summers said, and Mrs. Dunbar went steadily to   26
the box while one of the women said, "Go on, Janey," and another said, "There she goes."

"We're next," Mrs. Graves said. She watched while Mr. Graves   27
came around from the side of the box, greeted Mr. Summers gravely, and selected a slip of paper from the box. By now, all through the crowd there were men holding the small folded papers in their large hands, turning them over and over nervously. Mrs. Dunbar and her two sons stood together, Mrs. Dunbar holding the slip of paper.

"Harburt. . . . Hutchinson."   28

"Get up there, Bill," Mrs. Hutchinson said, and the people near   29
her laughed.

"Jones."   30

"They do say," Mr. Adams said to Old Man Warner, who stood   31
next to him, "that over in the north village they're talking of giving up the lottery."

Old Man Warner snorted. "Pack of crazy fools," he said.   32
"Listening to the young folks, nothing's good enough for *them*. Next thing you know, they'll be wanting to go back to living in caves, nobody work any more, live *that* way for a while. Used to be a saying about 'Lottery in June, corn be heavy soon.' First thing you know, we'd all be eating stewed chickweed and acorns. There's *always* been a lottery," he added petulantly. "Bad enough to see young Joe Summers up there joking with everybody."

"Some places have already quit lotteries," Mrs. Adams said.   33

"Nothing but trouble in *that*," Old Man Warner said stoutly.   34
"Pack of young fools."

"Martin." And Bobby Martin watched his father go forward.   35
"Overdyke. . . . Percy."

"I wish they'd hurry," Mrs. Dunbar said to her older son. "I wish 36
they'd hurry."

"They're almost through," her son said. 37

"You get ready to run tell Dad," Mrs. Dunbar said. 38

Mr. Summers called his own name and then stepped forward 39
precisely and selected a slip from the box. Then he called, "Warner."

"Seventy-seventh year I been in the lottery," Old Man Warner 40
said as he went through the crowd. "Seventy-seventh time."

"Watson." The tall boy came awkwardly through the crowd. 41
Someone said, "Don't be nervous, Jack," and Mr. Summers said,
"Take your time, son."

"Zanini." 42

After that, there was a long pause, a breathless pause, until Mr. 43
Summers, holding his slip of paper in the air, said, "All right, fellows." For a minute, no one moved, and then all the slips of paper
were opened. Suddenly, all the women began to speak at once, saying, "Who is it?" "Who's got it?" "Is it the Dunbars?" "Is it the
Watsons?" Then the voices began to say, "It's Hutchinson. It's Bill,"
"Bill Hutchinson's got it."

"Go tell your father," Mrs. Dunbar said to her older son. 44

People began to look around to see the Hutchinsons. Bill 45
Hutchinson was standing quiet, staring down at the paper in his
hand. Suddenly, Tessie Hutchinson shouted to Mr. Summers, "You
didn't give him time enough to take any paper he wanted. I saw you.
It wasn't fair!"

"Be a good sport, Tessie," Mrs. Delacroix called, and Mrs. Graves 46
said, "All of us took the same chance."

"Shut up, Tessie," Bill Hutchinson said. 47

"Well, everyone," Mr. Summers said, "that was done pretty fast, 48
and now we've got to be hurrying a little more to get done in time."
He consulted his next list. "Bill," he said, "you draw for the
Hutchinson family. You got any other households in the
Hutchinsons?"

"There's Don and Eva," Mrs. Hutchinson yelled. "Make *them* 49
take their chance!"

"Daughters draw with their husbands' families, Tessie," Mr. 50
Summers said gently. "You know that as well as anyone else."

"It wasn't *fair*," Tessie said. 51

"I guess not, Joe," Bill Hutchinson said regretfully. "My daugh- 52
ter draws with her husband's family, that's only fair. And I've got no
other family except the kids."

"Then, as far as drawing for families is concerned, it's you," Mr. [53] Summers said in explanation, "and as far as drawing for households is concerned, that's you, too. Right?"

"Right," Bill Hutchinson said. [54]

"How many kids, Bill?" Mr. Summers asked formally. [55]

"Three," Bill Hutchinson said. "There's Bill, Jr., and Nancy, and [56] little Dave. And Tessie and me."

"All right, then," Mr. Summers said. "Harry, you got their tickets [57] back?"

Mr. Graves nodded and held up the slips of paper. "Put them in [58] the box, then," Mr. Summers directed. "Take Bill's and put it in."

"I think we ought to start over," Mrs. Hutchinson said, as quietly [59] as she could. "I tell you it wasn't *fair*. You didn't give him time enough to choose. *Every*body saw that."

Mr. Graves had selected the five slips and put them in the box, [60] and he dropped all the papers but those onto the ground, where the breeze caught them and lifted them off.

"Listen, everybody," Mrs. Hutchinson was saying to the people [61] around her.

"Ready, Bill?" Mr. Summers asked, and Bill Hutchinson, with [62] one quick glance around at his wife and children, nodded.

"Remember," Mr. Summers said, "take the slips and keep them [63] folded until each person has taken one. Harry, you help little Dave." Mr. Graves took the hand of the little boy, who came willingly with him up to the box. "Take a paper out of the box, Davy," Mr. Summers said. Davy put his hand into the box and laughed. "Take just *one* paper," Mr. Summers said. "Harry, you hold it for him." Mr. Graves took the child's hand and removed the folded paper from the tight fist and held it while little Dave stood next to him and looked up at him wonderingly.

"Nancy next," Mr. Summers said. Nancy was twelve, and her [64] school friends breathed heavily as she went forward, switching her skirt, and took a slip daintily from the box. "Bill, Jr.," Mr. Summers said, and Billy, his face red and his feet over-large, nearly knocked the box over as he got a paper out. "Tessie," Mr. Summers said. She hesitated for a minute, looking around defiantly, and then set her lips and went up to the box. She snatched a paper out and held it behind her.

"Bill," Mr. Summers said, and Bill Hutchinson reached into the [65] box and felt around, bringing his hand out at last with the slip of paper in it.

The crowd was quiet. A girl whispered, "I hope it's not Nancy," 66
and the sound of the whisper reached the edges of the crowd.

"It's not the way it used to be," Old Man Warner said clearly. 67
"People ain't they way they used to be."

"All right," Mr. Summers said. "Open the papers. Harry, you 68
open little Dave's."

Mr. Graves opened the slip of paper and there was a general sigh 69
through the crowd as he held it up and everyone could see that it was
blank. Nancy and Bill, Jr., opened theirs at the same time, and both
beamed and laughed, turning around to the crowd and holding their
slips of paper above their heads.

"Tessie," Mr. Summers said. There was a pause, and then Mr. 70
Summers looked at Bill Hutchinson, and Bill unfolded his paper and
showed it. It was blank.

"It's Tessie," Mr. Summers said, and his voice was hushed. 71
"Show us her paper, Bill."

Bill Hutchinson went over to his wife and forced the slip of paper 72
out of her hand. It had a black spot on it, the black spot Mr. Summers
had made the night before with the heavy pencil in the coal-company
office. Bill Hutchinson held it up, and there was a stir in the crowd.

"All right, folks," Mr. Summers said. "Let's finish quickly." 73

Although the villagers had forgotten the ritual and lost the orig- 74
inal black box, they still remembered to use stones. The pile of stones
the boys had made earlier was ready; there were stones on the
ground with the blowing scraps of paper that had come out of the
box. Mrs. Delacroix selected a stone so large she had to pick it up
with both hands and turned to Mrs. Dunbar. "Come on," she said.
"Hurry up."

Mrs. Dunbar had small stones in both hands, and she said, gasp- 75
ing for breath, "I can't run at all. You'll have to go ahead and I'll catch
up with you."

The children had stones already, and someone gave little Davy 76
Hutchinson a few pebbles.

Tessie Hutchinson was in the center of a cleared space by now, 77
and she held her hands out desperately as the villagers moved in on
her. "It isn't fair," she said. A stone hit her on the side of the head.

Old Man Warner was saying, "Come on, come on, everyone." 78
Steve Adams was in the front of the crowd of villagers with Mrs.
Graves beside him.

"It isn't fair, it isn't right," Mrs. Hutchinson screamed, and then 79
they were upon her.

A & P[1]

John Updike

In walks these three girls in nothing but bathing suits. I'm in the 1
third checkout slot, with my back to the door, so I don't see them
until they're over by the bread. The one that caught my eye first was
the one in the plaid green two-piece. She was a chunky kid, with a
good tan and a sweet broad soft-looking can with those two crescents
of white just under it, where the sun never seems to hit, at the top of
the backs of her legs. I stood there with my hand on a box of HiHo
crackers trying to remember if I rang it up or not. I ring it up again
and the customer starts giving me hell. She's one of these cash-regis-
ter-watchers, a witch about fifty with rouge on her cheekbones and
no eyebrows, and I know it made her day to trip me up. She'd been
watching cash registers for fifty years and probably never seen a mistake before.

By the time I got her feathers smoothed and her goodies into a 2
bag—she gives me a little snort in passing, if she'd been born at the
right time they would have burned her over in Salem—by the time I
get her on her way the girls had circled around the bread and were
coming back, without a pushcart, back my way along the counters, in
the aisle between the checkouts and the Special bins. They didn't
even have shoes on. There was this chunky one, with the two-piece—
it was bright green and the seams on the bra were still sharp and her
belly was still pretty pale so I guessed she just got it (the suit)—there
was this one, with one of those chubby berry-faces, the lips all
bunched together under her nose, this one, and a tall one, with black
hair that hadn't quite frizzed right, and one of these sunburns right
across under the eyes, and a chin that was too long—you know, the
kind of girl other girls think is very "striking" and "attractive" but
never quite makes it, as they very well know, which is why they like
her so much—and then the third one, that wasn't quite so tall. She
was the queen. She kind of led them, the other two peeking around
and making their shoulders round. She didn't look around, not this
queen, she just walked straight on slowly, on these long white prima-
donna legs. She came down a little hard on her heels, as if she didn't
walk in her bare feet that much, putting down her heels and then let-

---

[1] *A & P:* the Great Atlantic and Pacific Tea Company, a large grocery chain established in 1859
and still flourishing in 18 states, with more than 800 A & P stores in the United States and 200
in Canada.

ting the weight move along to her toes as if she was testing the floor
with every step, putting a little deliberate extra action into it. You
never know for sure how girls' minds work (do you really think it's
a mind in there or just a little buzz like a bee in a glass jar?) but you
got the idea she had talked the other two into coming in here with
her, and now she was showing them how to do it, walk slow and
hold yourself straight.

She had on a kind of dirty-pink—beige, maybe, I don't know—   3
bathing suit with a little nubble all over it and, what got me, the
straps were down. They were off her shoulders looped loose around
the cool tops of her arms, and I guess as a result the suit had slipped
a little on her, so all around the top of the cloth there was this shining
rim. If it hadn't been there you wouldn't have known there could
have been anything whiter than those shoulders. With the straps
pushed off, there was nothing between the top of the suit and the top
of her head except just *her*, this clean bare plane of the top of her chest
down from the shoulder bones like a dented sheet of metal tilted in
the light. I mean, it was more than pretty.

She had sort of oaky hair that the sun and salt had bleached,   4
done up in a bun that was unraveling, and a kind of prim face.
Walking into the A & P with your straps down, I suppose it's the only
kind of face you *can* have. She held her head so high her neck, coming up out of those white shoulders, looked kind of stretched, but I
didn't mind. The longer her neck was, the more of her there was.

She must have felt in the corner of her eye me and over my   5
shoulder Stokesie in the second slot watching, but she didn't tip. Not
this queen. She kept her eyes moving across the racks, and stopped,
and turned so slow it made my stomach rub the inside of my apron,
and buzzed to the other two, who kind of huddled against her for
relief, and then they all three of them went up the cat-and-dog-food-
breakfast-cereal-macaroni-rice-raisins-seasonings-spreads-spaghetti-
soft-drinks-crackers-and-cookies aisle. From the third slot I look
straight up this aisle to the meat counter, and I watched them all the
way. The fat one with the tan sort of fumbled with the cookies, but on
second thought she put the package back. The sheep pushing their
carts down the aisle—the girls were walking against the usual traffic
(not that we have one-way signs or anything)—were pretty hilarious.
You could see them, when Queenie's white shoulders dawned on
them, kind of jerk, or hop, or hiccup, but their eyes snapped back to
their own baskets and on they pushed. I bet you could set off dynamite in an A & P and the people would by and large keep reaching
and checking oatmeal off their lists and muttering "Let me see, there

was a third thing, began with A, asparagus, no ah, yes, applesauce!" or whatever it is they do mutter. But there was no doubt, this jiggled them. A few houseslaves in pin curlers even looked around after pushing their carts past to make sure what they had seen was correct.

You know, it's one thing to have a girl in a bathing suit down on 6 the beach, where what with the glare nobody can look at each other much anyway, and another thing in the cool of the A & P, under the fluorescent lights, against all those stacked packages, with her feet paddling along naked over our checkerboard green-and-cream rubber-tile floor.

"Oh Daddy," Stokesie said beside me. "I feel so faint." 7

"Darling," I said. "Hold me tight." Stokesie's married, with two 8 babies chalked up on his fuselage already, but as far as I can tell that's the only difference. He's twenty-two, and I was nineteen this April.

"Is it done?" he asks, the responsible married man finding his 9 voice. I forgot to say he thinks he's going to be manager some sunny day, maybe in 1990 when it's called the Great Alexandrov and Petrooshki[2] Tea Company or something.

What he meant was, our town is five miles from the beach, with 10 a big summer colony out on the Point, but we're right in the middle of town, and the women generally put on a shirt or shorts or something before they get out of the car into the street. And anyway these are usually women with six children and varicose veins mapping their legs and nobody, including them, could care less. As I say, we're right in the middle of town, and if you stand at our front doors you can see two banks and the Congregational church and the newspaper store and three real-estate offices and about twenty-seven old freeloaders tearing up Central Street because the sewer broke again. It's not as if we're on the Cape,[3] we're north of Boston and there's people in this town haven't seen the ocean for twenty years.

The girls had reached the meat counter and were asking 11 McMahon something. He pointed, they pointed, and they shuffled out of sight behind a pyramid of Diet Delight peaches. All that was left for us to see was old McMahon patting his mouth and looking after them sizing up their joints. Poor kids, I began to feel sorry for them, they couldn't help it.

---

[2] Great Alexandrov and Petrooshki: apparently a reference to the possibility that someday Russia might rule the United States.

[3] the Cape: Cape Cod, the southeastern area of Massachusetts, a place of many resorts and beaches.

Now here comes the sad part of the story, at least my family says 12
it's sad, but I don't think it's so sad myself. The store's pretty empty, it
being Thursday afternoon, so there was nothing much to do except
lean on the register and wait for the girls to show up again. The whole
store was like a pinball machine and I didn't know which tunnel
they'd come out of. After a while they come around out of the far aisle,
around the light bulbs, records at discount of the Caribbean Six or
Tony Martin Sings or some such gunk you wonder they waste the wax
on, sixpacks of candy bars, and plastic toys done up in cellophane that
fall apart when a kid looks at them anyway. Around they come,
Queenie still leading the way, and holding a little gray jar in her hand.
Slots Three through Seven are unmanned and I could see her wondering between Stokes and me, but Stokesie with his usual luck draws an
old party in baggy gray pants who stumbles up with four giant cans of
pineapple juice (what do these bums *do* with all that pineapple juice?
I've often asked myself) so the girls come to me. Queenie puts down
the jar and I take it into my fingers icy cold. Kingfish Fancy Herring
Snacks in Pure Sour Cream: 49¢. Now her hands are empty, not a ring
or a bracelet, bare as God made them, and I wonder where the
money's coming from. Still with that prim look she lifts a folded dol-
lar bill out of the hollow at the center of her nubbed pink top. The jar
went heavy in my hand. Really, I thought that was so cute.

Then everybody's luck begins to run out. Lengel comes in from 13
haggling with a truck full of cabbages on the lot and is about to scut-
tle into that door marked MANAGER behind which he hides all day
when the girls touch his eye. Lengel's pretty dreary, teaches Sunday
school and the rest, but he doesn't miss that much. He comes over
and says, "Girls, this isn't the beach."

Queenie blushes, though maybe it's just a brush of sunburn I was 14
noticing for the first time, now that she was so close. "My mother
asked me to pick up a jar of herring snacks." Her voice kind of startled me, the way voices do when you see the people first, coming out
so flat and dumb yet kind of tony, too, the way it ticked over "pick
up" and "snacks." All of a sudden I slid right down her voice into her
living room. Her father and the other men were standing around in
ice-cream coats and bow ties and the women were in sandals picking
up herring snacks on toothpicks off a big glass plate and they were
all holding drinks the color of water with olives and sprigs of mint in
them. When my parents have somebody over they get lemonade and
if it's a real racy affair Schlitz in tall glasses with "They'll Do It Every
Time"[4] cartoons stenciled on.

---

[4] *They'll Do It Every Time*": syndicated daily and Sunday cartoon created by Jimmy Hatlo.

"That's all right," Lengel said. "But this isn't the beach." His 15
repeating this struck me as funny, as if it had just occurred to him,
and he had been thinking all these years the A & P was a great big
dune and he was the head lifeguard. He didn't like my smiling—as I
say he doesn't miss much—but he concentrates on giving the girls
that sad Sunday-school-superintendent stare.

Queenie's blush is no sunburn now, and the plump one in plaid, 16
that I liked better from the back—a really sweet can—pipes up, "We
weren't doing any shopping. We just came in for the one thing."

"That makes no difference," Lengel tells her, and I could see from 17
the way his eyes went that he hadn't noticed she was wearing a two-
piece before. "We want you decently dressed when you come in here."

"We *are* decent," Queenie says suddenly, her lower lip pushing, 18
getting sore now that she remembers her place, a place from which
the crowd that runs the A & P must look pretty crummy. Fancy
Herring Snacks flashed in her very blue eyes.

"Girls, I don't want to argue with you. After this come in here 19
with your shoulders covered. It's our policy." He turns his back.
That's policy for you. Policy is what the kingpins want. What the others want is juvenile delinquency.

All this while, the customers had been showing up with their 20
carts but, you know, sheep, seeing a scene, they had all bunched up
on Stokesie, who shook open a paper bag as gently as peeling a
peach, not wanting to miss a word. I could feel in the silence everybody getting nervous, most of all Lengel, who asks me, "Sammy,
have you rung up their purchase?"

I thought and said "No" but it wasn't about that I was thinking. 21
I go through the punches, 4, 9, GROC, TOT—it's more complicated than
you think, and after you do it often enough, it begins to make a little
song, that you hear words to, in my case "Hello (>*bing*) there, you
(*gung*) hap-py *pee*-pul (*splat*)!"—the *splat* being the drawer flying out.
I uncrease the bill, tenderly as you may imagine, it just having come
from between the two smoothest scoops of vanilla I had ever known
were there, and pass a half and a penny into her narrow pink palm,
and nestle the herrings in a bag and twist its neck and hand it over,
all the time thinking.

The girls, and who'd blame them, are in a hurry to get out, so I 22
say "I quit" to Lengel quick enough for them to hear, hoping they'll
stop and watch me, their unsuspected hero. They keep right on
going, into the electric eye; the door flies open and they flicker across
the lot to their car, Queenie and Plaid and Big Tall Goony-Goony (not

that as raw material she was so bad), leaving me with Lengel and a kink in his eyebrow.

"Did you say something, Sammy?"   23

"I said I quit."   24

"I thought you did."   25

"You didn't have to embarrass them."   26

"It was they who were embarrassing us."   27

I started to say something that came out "Fiddle-de-doo." It's a 28 saying of my grandmother's, and I know she would have been pleased.

"I don't think you know what you're saying," Lengel said.   29

"I know you don't," I said. "But I do." I pull the bow at the back 30 of my apron and start shrugging it off my shoulders. A couple customers that had been heading for my slot begin to knock against each other, like scared pigs in a chute.

Lengel sighs and begins to look very patient and old and gray. 31 He's been a friend of my parents for years. "Sammy, you don't want to do this to your Mom and Dad," he tells me. It's true, I don't. But it seems to me that once you begin a gesture it's fatal not to go through with it. I fold the apron, "Sammy" stitched in red on the pocket, and put it on the counter, and drop the bow tie on top of it. The bow tie is theirs, if you've ever wondered. "You'll feel this for the rest of your life," Lengel says, and I know that's true, too, but remembering how he made that pretty girl blush makes me so scrunchy inside I punch the No Sale tab and the machine whirs "pee-pul" and the drawer splats out. One advantage to this scene taking place in summer, I can follow this up with a clean exit, there's no fumbling around getting your coat and galoshes, I just saunter into the electric eye in my white shirt that my mother ironed the night before, and the door heaves itself open, and outside the sunshine is skating around on the asphalt.

I look around for my girls, but they're gone, of course. There 32 wasn't anybody but some young married screaming with her children about some candy they didn't get by the door of a powder-blue Falcon[5] station wagon. Looking back in the big windows, over the bags of peat moss and aluminum lawn furniture stacked on the pavement, I could see Lengel in my place in the slot, checking the sheep through. His face was dark gray and his back stiff, as if he'd just had an injection of iron, and my stomach kind of fell as I felt how hard the world was going to be to me hereafter.

---

[5] *Falcon:* small car that had recently been introduced by the Ford Motor Company.

THE CHRYSANTHEMUMS

John Steinbeck

The high grey-flannel fog of winter closed off the Salinas Valley[1] from the sky and from all the rest of the world. On every side it sat like a lid on the mountains and made of the great valley a closed pot. On the broad, level land floor the gang plows bit deep and left the black earth shining like metal where the shares had cut. On the foothill ranches across the Salinas River, the yellow stubble fields seemed to be bathed in pale cold sunshine, but there was no sunshine in the valley now in December. The thick willow scrub along the river flamed with sharp and positive yellow leaves.

It was a time of quiet and of waiting. The air was cold and tender. A light wind blew up from the southwest so that the farmers were mildly hopeful of a good rain before long; but fog and rain do not go together.

Across the river, on Henry Allen's foothill ranch there was little work to be done, for the hay was cut and stored and the orchards were plowed up to receive the rain deeply when it should come. The cattle on the higher slopes were becoming shaggy and rough-coated.

Elisa Allen, working in her flower garden, looked down across the yard and saw Henry, her husband, talking to two men in business suits. The three of them stood by the tractor shed, each man with one foot on the side of the little Fordson.[2] They smoked cigarettes and studied the machines as they talked.

Elisa watched them for a moment and then went back to her work. She was thirty-five. Her face was lean and strong and her eyes were as clear as water. Her figure looked blocked and heavy in her gardening costume, a man's black hat pulled low down over her eyes, clodhopper shoes, a figured print dress almost completely covered by a big corduroy apron with four big pockets to hold the snips, the trowel and scratcher, the seeds and the knife she worked with. She wore heavy leather gloves to protect her hands while she worked.

She was cutting down the old year's chrysanthemum stalks with a pair of short and powerful scissors. She looked down toward the men by the tractor shed now and then. Her face was eager and

---

[1] *Salinas Valley:* in Monterey County, California, about 50 miles south of San Jose.
[2] Fordson: a tractor manufactured by the Ford Motor Company, with large steel-lugged rear wheels.

mature and handsome; even her work with the scissors was over-eager, over-powerful. The chrysanthemum stems seemed too small and easy for her energy.

She brushed a cloud of hair out of her eyes with the back of her   7
glove, and left a smudge of earth on the cheek in doing it. Behind her stood the neat white farm house with red geraniums close-banked around it as high as the windows. It was a hard-swept looking little house, with hard-polished windows, and a clean mud-mat on the front steps.

Elisa cast another glance toward the tractor shed. The strangers   8
were getting into their Ford coupe. She took off a glove and put her strong fingers down into the forest of new green chrysanthemum sprouts that were growing around the old roots. She spread the leaves and looked down among the close-growing stems. No aphids were there, no sowbugs or snails or cutworms. Her terrier fingers destroyed such pests before they could get started.

Elisa started at the sound of her husband's voice. He had come   9
near quietly, and he leaned over the wire fence that protected her flower garden from cattle and dogs and chickens. "At it again," he said. "You've got a strong new crop coming."   10

Elisa straightened her back and pulled on the gardening glove   11
again. "Yes. They'll be strong this coming year." In her tone and on her face there was a little smugness.

"You've got a gift with things," Henry observed. "Some of those   12
yellow chrysanthemums you had this year were ten inches across. I wish you'd work out in the orchard and raise some apples that big."

Her eyes sharpened. "Maybe I could do it, too. I've a gift with   13
things, all right. My mother had it. She could stick anything in the ground and make it grow. She said it was having planters' hands that knew how to do it."

"Well, it sure works with flowers," he said.   14

"Henry, who were those men you were talking to?"   15

"Why, sure, that's what I came to tell you. They were from the   16
Western Meat Company. I sold those thirty head of three-year-old steers. Got nearly my own price, too."

"Good," she said. "Good for you."   17

"And I thought," he continued, "I thought how it's Saturday   18
afternoon, and we might go to Salinas for dinner at a restaurant, and then to a picture show—to celebrate, you see."

"Good," she repeated. "Oh, yes. That will be good."   19

Henry put on his joking tone. "There's fights tonight. How'd you   20
like to go to the fights?"

"Oh, no," she said breathlessly. "No, I wouldn't like fights."   21
"Just fooling, Elisa. We'll go to a movie. Let's see. It's two now.   22
I'm going to take Scotty and bring down those steers from the hill.
It'll take us maybe two hours. We'll go in town about five and have
dinner at the Cominos Hotel. Like that?"

"Of course I'll like it. It's good to eat away from home."   23

"All right, then. I'll go get up a couple of horses."   24

She said, "I'll have plenty of time to transplant some of these sets,   25
I guess."

She heard her husband calling Scotty down by the barn. And a   26
little later she saw the two men ride up the pale yellow hillside in
search of the steers.

There was a little square sandy bed kept for rooting the chrysan-   27
themums. With her trowel she turned the soil over and over, and
smoothed it and patted it firm. Then she dug ten parallel trenches to
receive the sets. Back at the chrysanthemum bed she pulled out the
little crisp shoots, trimmed off the leaves of each one with her scissors and laid it on a small orderly pile.

A squeak of wheels and plod of hoofs came from the road. Elisa   28
looked up. The country road ran along the dense bank of willows
and cottonwoods that bordered the river, and up this road came a
curious vehicle, curiously drawn. It was an old springwagon, with a
round canvas top on it like the cover of a prairie schooner. It was
drawn by an old bay horse and a little grey-and-white burro. A big
stubble-bearded man sat between the cover flaps and drove the
crawling team. Underneath the wagon, between the hind wheels, a
lean and rangy mongrel dog walked sedately. Words were painted on
the canvas in clumsy, crooked letters. "Pots, pans, knives, sisors,
lawn mores. Fixed." Two rows of articles and the triumphantly defin-
itive "Fixed" below. The black paint had run down in little sharp
points beneath each letter.

Elisa, squatting on the ground, watched to see the crazy, loose-   29
jointed wagon pass by. But it didn't pass. It turned into the farm road
in front of her house, crooked old wheels skirling and squeaking. The
rangy dog darted from between the wheels and ran ahead. Instantly
the two ranch shepherds flew out at him. Then all three stopped, and
with stiff and quivering tails, with taut straight legs, with ambas-
sadorial dignity, they slowly circled, sniffing daintily. The caravan
pulled up to Elisa's wire fence and stopped. Now the newcomer dog,
feeling outnumbered, lowered his tail and retired under the wagon
with raised hackles and bared teeth.

The man on the wagon seat called out. "That's a bad dog in a ₃₀
fight when he gets started."

Elisa laughed. "I see he is. How soon does he generally get ₃₁
started?"

The man caught up her laughter and echoed it heartily. ₃₂
"Sometimes not for weeks and weeks," he said. He climbed stiffly
down, over the wheel. The horse and the donkey dropped like unwa-
tered flowers.

Elisa saw that he was a very big man. Although his hair and beard ₃₃
were greying, he did not look old. His worn black suit was wrinkled
and spotted with grease. The laughter had disappeared from his face
and eyes the moment his laughing voice ceased. His eyes were dark
and they were full of the brooding that gets in the eyes of teamsters and
of sailors. The calloused hands he rested on the wire fence were
cracked, and every crack was a black line. He took off his battered hat.

"I'm off my general road, ma'am," he said. "Does this dirt road ₃₄
cut over across the river to the Los Angeles highway?"

Elisa stood up and shoved the thick scissors in her apron pocket. ₃₅
"Well, yes, it does, but it winds around and then fords the river. I
don't think your team could pull through the sand."

He replied with some asperity, "It might surprise you what them ₃₆
beasts can pull through."

"When they get started?" she asked. ₃₇

He smiled for a second. "Yes. When they get started." ₃₈

"Well," said Elisa, "I think you'll save time if you go back to the ₃₉
Salinas road and pick up the highway there."

He drew a big finger down the chicken wire and made it sing. "I ₄₀
ain't in any hurry, ma'am. I go from Seattle to San Diego and back
every year. Takes all my time. About six months each way. I aim to
follow nice weather."

Elisa took off her gloves and stuffed them in the apron pocket ₄₁
with the scissors. She touched the under edge of her man's hat,
searching for fugitive hairs. "That sounds like a nice kind of a way to
live," she said.

He leaned confidentially over the fence. "Maybe you noticed the ₄₂
writing on my wagon. I mend pots and sharpen knives and scissors.
You got any of them things to do?"

"Oh, no," she said quickly. "Nothing like that." Her eyes hard- ₄₃
ened with resistance.

"Scissors is the worst thing," he explained. "Most people just ₄₄
ruin scissors trying to sharpen 'em, but I know how. I got a special

tool. It's a little bobbit kind of thing, and patented. But it sure does the trick."

"No. My scissors are all sharp."   45

"All right, then. Take a pot," he continued earnestly, "a bent pot,   46
or a pot with a hole. I can make it like new so you don't have to buy
no new ones. That's saving for you."

"No," she said shortly. "I tell you I have nothing like that for you   47
to do."

His face fell to an exaggerated sadness. His voice took on a whin-   48
ing undertone. "I ain't had a thing to do today. Maybe I won't have
no supper tonight. You see I'm off my regular road. I know folks on
the highway clear from Seattle to San Diego. They save their things
for me to sharpen up because they know I do it so good and save
them money."

"I'm sorry," Elisa said irritably. "I haven't anything for you   49
to do."

His eyes left her face and fell to searching the ground. They   50
roamed about until they came to the chrysanthemum bed where she
had been working. "What's them plants, ma'am?"

The irritation and resistance melted from Elisa's face. "Oh, those   51
are chrysanthemums, giant whites and yellows. I raise them every
year, bigger than anybody around here."

"Kind of a long-stemmed flower? Looks like a quick puff of col-   52
ored smoke?" he asked.

"That's it. What a nice way to describe them."   53

"They smell kind of nasty till you get used to them," he said.   54

"It's a good bitter smell," she retorted, "not nasty at all."   55

He changed his tone quickly. "I like the smell myself."   56

"I had ten-inch blooms this year," she said.   57

The man leaned farther over the fence. "Look. I know a lady down   58
the road a piece, has got the nicest garden you ever seen. Got nearly
every kind of flower but no chrysantheums. Last time I was mending
a copper-bottom washtub for her (that's hard job but I do it good), she
said to me, 'If you ever run acrost some nice chrysantheums I wish
you'd try to get me a few seeds.' That's what she told me."

Elisa's eyes grew alert and eager. "She couldn't have known   59
much about chrysanthemums. You can raise them from seed, but it's
much easier to root the little sprouts you see there."

"Oh," he said. "I s'pose I can't take none to her, then."   60

"Why yes you can," Elisa cried. "I can put some in damp sand,
and you can carry them right along with you. They'll take root in the
pot if you keep them damp. And then she can transplant them."

"She'd sure like to have some, ma'am. You say they're nice ones?" 62
"Beautiful," she said. "Oh, beautiful." Her eyes shone. She tore off 63
the battered hat and shook out her dark pretty hair. "I'll put them in a
flower pot, and you can take them right with you. Come into the yard."
While the man came through the picket gate Elisa ran excitedly 64
along the geranium-bordered path to the back of the house. And she
returned carrying a big red flower pot. The gloves were forgotten
now. She kneeled on the ground by the starting bed and dug up the
sandy soil with her fingers and scooped it into the bright new flower
pot. Then she picked up the little pile of shoots she had prepared.
With her strong fingers she pressed them into the sand and tamped
around them with her knuckles. The man stood over her. "I'll tell you
what to do," she said. "You remember so you can tell the lady."

"Yes, I'll try to remember." 65

"Well, look. These will take root in about a month. Then she must 66
set them out, about a foot apart in good rich earth like this, see?" She
lifted a handful of dark soil for him to look at. "They'll grow fast and
tall. Now remember this. In July tell her to cut them down, about
eight inches from the ground."

"Before they bloom?" he asked. 67

"Yes, before they bloom." Her face was tight with eagerness. 68
"They'll grow right up again. About the last of September the buds
will start."

She stopped and seemed perplexed. "It's the budding that takes 69
the most care," she said hesitantly. "I don't know how to tell you."
She looked deep into his eyes, searchingly. Her mouth opened a little, and she seemed to be listening. "I'll try to tell you," she said. "Did
you ever hear of planting hands?"

"Can't say I have, ma'am." 70

"Well, I can only tell you what it feels like. It's when you're pick- 71
ing off the buds you don't want. Everything goes right down into
your fingertips. You watch your fingers work. They do it themselves.
You can feel how it is. They pick and pick the buds. They never make
a mistake. They're with the plant. Do you see? Your fingers and the
plant. You can feel that, right up your arm. They know. They never
make a mistake. You can feel it. When you're like that you can't do
anything wrong. Do you see that? Can you understand that?"

She was kneeling on the ground looking up at him. Her breast 72
swelled passionately.

The man's eyes narrowed. He looked away self-consciously. 73
"Maybe I know," he said. "Sometimes in the night in the wagon
there—"

Elisa's voice grew husky. She broke in on him. "I've never lived   74
as you do, but I know what you mean. When the night is dark—why,
the stars are sharp-pointed, and there's quiet. Why, you rise up and
up! Every pointed star gets driven into your body. It's like that. Hot
and sharp and—lovely."

Kneeling there, her hand went out toward his legs in the greasy   75
black trousers. Her hesitant fingers almost touched the cloth. Then
her hand dropped to the ground. She crouched low like a fawning
dog.

He said, "It's nice, just like you say. Only when you don't have   76
no dinner, it ain't."

She stood up then, very straight, and her face was ashamed. She   77
held the flower pot out to him and placed it gently in his arms. "Here.
Put it in your wagon, on the seat, where you can watch it. Maybe I
can find something for you to do."

At the back of the house she dug in the can pile and found two   78
old and battered aluminum saucepans. She carried them back and
gave them to him. "Here, maybe you can fix these."

His manner changed. He became professional. "Good as new I   79
can fix them." At the back of his wagon he set a little anvil, and out
of an oily tool box dug a small machine hammer. Elisa came through
the gate to watch him while he pounded out the dents in the kettles.
His mouth grew sure and knowing. At a difficult part of the work he
sucked his under-lip.

"You sleep right in the wagon?" Elisa asked.   80

"Right in the wagon, ma'am. Rain or shine. I'm dry as a cow in   81
there."

"It must be nice," she said. "It must be very nice. I wish women   82
could do such things."

"It ain't the right kind of a life for a woman."   83

Her upper lip raised a little, showing her teeth. "How do you   84
know? How can you tell?" she said.

"I don't know ma'am," he protested. "Of course I don't know.   85
Now here's your kettles, done. You don't have to buy no new ones."

"How much?"   86

"Oh, fifty cents'll do. I keep my prices down and my work good.   87
That's why I have all them satisfied customers up and down the
highway."

Elisa brought him a fifty-cent piece from the house and dropped   88
it in his hand. "You might be surprised to have a rival some time. I
can sharpen scissors, too. And I can beat the dents out of little pots. I
could show you what a woman might do."

He put his hammer back in the oily box and shoved the little 89 anvil out of sight. "It would be a lonely life for a woman, ma'am, and a scarey life, too, with animals creeping under the wagon all night." He climbed over the single-tree, steadying himself with a hand on the burro's white rump. He settled himself in the seat, picked up the lines. "Thank you kindly, ma'am," he said. "I'll do like you told me; I'll go back and catch the Salinas road."

"Mind," she called, "if you're long in getting there, keep the sand 90 damp."

"Sand, ma'am? . . . Sand? Oh, sure. You mean round the chrysan- 91 theums. Sure I will." He clucked his tongue. The beasts leaned luxuriously into their collars. The mongrel dog took his place between the back wheels. The wagon turned and crawled out the entrance road and back the way it had come, along the river.

Elisa stood in front of her wire fence watching the slow progress 92 of the caravan. Her shoulders were straight, her head thrown back, her eyes half-closed, so that the scene came vaguely into them. Her lips moved silently, forming the words "Good-bye—good-bye." Then she whispered, "That's a bright direction. There's a glowing there." The sound of her whisper startled her. She shook herself free and looked about to see whether anyone had been listening. Only the dogs had heard. They lifted their heads toward her from their sleeping in the dust, and then stretched out their chins and settled asleep again. Elisa turned and ran hurriedly into the house.

In the kitchen she reached behind the stove and felt the water 93 tank. It was full of hot water from the noonday cooking. In the bathroom she tore off her soiled clothes and flung them into the corner. And then she scrubbed herself with a little block of pumice, legs and thighs, loins and chest and arms, until her skin was scratched and red. When she had dried herself she stood in front of a mirror in her bedroom and looked at her body. She tightened her stomach and threw out her chest. She turned and looked over her shoulder at her back.

After a while she began to dress, slowly. She put on her newest 94 under-clothing and her nicest stockings and the dress which was the symbol of her prettiness. She worked carefully on her hair, pencilled her eyebrows and rouged her lips.

Before she was finished she heard the little thunder of hoofs and 95 the shouts of Henry and his helper as they drove the red steers into the corral. She heard the gate bang shut and set herself for Henry's arrival.

His step sounded on the porch. He entered the house calling 96 "Elisa, where are you?"

"In my room, dressing. I'm not ready. There's hot water for your 97 bath. Hurry up. It's getting late."

When she heard him splashing in the tub, Elisa laid his dark suit 98 on the bed, and shirt and socks and tie beside it. She stood his polished shoes on the floor beside the bed. Then she went to the porch and sat primly and stiffly down. She looked toward the river road where the willow-line was still yellow with frosted leaves so that under the high grey fog they seemed a thin band of sunshine. This was the only color in the grey afternoon. She sat unmoving for a long time. Her eyes blinked rarely.

Henry came banging out of the door, shoving his tie inside his 99 vest as he came. Elisa stiffened and her face grew tight. Henry stopped short and looked at her. "Why—why, Elisa. You look so nice!"

"Nice? You think I look nice? What do you mean by 'nice'?" 100

Henry blundered on. "I don't know. I mean you look different, 101 strong and happy."

"I am strong? Yes, strong. What do you mean 'strong'?" 102

He looked bewildered. "You're playing some kind of a game," he 103 said helplessly. "It's a kind of a play. You look strong enough to break a calf over your knee, happy enough to eat it like watermelon."

For a second she lost her rigidity. "Henry! Don't talk like that. 104 You didn't know what you said." She grew complete again. "I'm strong," she boasted. "I never knew before how strong."

Henry looked down toward the tractor shed, and when he 105 brought his eyes back to her, they were his own again. "I'll get out the car. You can put on your coat while I'm starting."

Elisa went into the house. She heard him drive to the gate and 106 idle down his motor, and then she took a long time to put on her hat. She pulled it here and pressed it there. When Henry turned the motor off she slipped into her coat and went out.

The little roadster bounced along on the dirt road by the river, 107 raising the birds and driving the rabbits into the brush. Two cranes flapped heavily over the willow-line and dropped into the river-bed.

Far ahead on the road Elisa saw a dark speck. She knew. 108

She tried not to look as they passed it, but her eyes would not 109 obey. She whispered to herself sadly. "He might have thrown them off the road. That wouldn't have been much trouble, not very much. But he kept the pot," she explained. "He had to keep the pot. That's why he couldn't get them off the road."

The roadster turned a bend and she saw the caravan ahead. She 110 swung full around toward her husband so she could not see the little covered wagon and the mismatched team as the car passed them. In a moment it was over. The thing was done. She did not look 111 back. She said loudly, to be heard above the motor, "It will be good, tonight, a good dinner."

"Now you're changed again," Henry complained. He took one 112 hand from the wheel and patted her knee. "I ought to take you in to dinner oftener. It would be good for both of us. We get so heavy out on the ranch."

"Henry," she asked, "could we have wine at dinner?"   113

"Sure we could. Say! That will be fine."   114

She was silent for a little while; then she said, "Henry, at those 115 prize fights, do the men hurt each other very much?"

"Sometimes a little, not often. Why?"   116

"Well, I've read how they break noses, and blood runs down 117 their chests. I've read how the fighting gloves get heavy and soggy with blood."

He looked around at her. "What's the matter, Elisa? I didn't 118 know you read things like that." He brought the car to a stop, then turned to the right over the Salinas River bridge.

"Do any women ever go to the fights?" she asked.   119

"Oh, sure, some. What's the matter, Elisa? Do you want to go? I 120 don't think you'd like it, but I'll take you if you really want to go."

She relaxed limply in the seat. "Oh, no. No. I don't want to go. 121 I'm sure I don't." Her face was turned away from him. "It will be enough if we can have wine. It will be plenty." She turned up her coat collar so he could not see that she was crying weakly—like an old woman.

ROMAN FEVER

Edith Wharton

From the table at which they had been lunching two American 1
ladies of ripe but well-cared-for middle age moved across the lofty
terrace of the Roman restaurant and, leaning on its parapet, looked
first at each other, and then down on the outspread glories of the
Palatine and the Forum, with the same expression of vague but
benevolent approval

As they leaned there a girlish voice echoed up gaily from the 2
stairs leading to the court below. "Well, come along, then," it cried,
not to them but to an invisible companion, "and let's leave the young
things to their knitting;" and a voice as fresh laughed back: "Oh, look
here, Babs, not actually *knitting*—" "Well, I mean figuratively,"
rejoined the first. "After all, we haven't left our poor parents much
else to do . . ." and at that point the turn of the stairs engulfed the
dialogue.

The two ladies looked at each other again, this time with a tinge 3
of smiling embarrassment, and the smaller and paler one shook her
head and colored—slightly.

"Barbara!" she murmured, sending an unheard rebuke after the 4
mocking voice in the stairway.

The other lady, who was fuller, and higher in color, with a small 5
determined nose supported by vigorous black eyebrows, gave a
good-humored laugh. "That's what our daughters think of us!"

Her companion replied by a deprecating gesture. "Not of us indi- 6
vidually. We must remember that. It's just the collective modern idea
of Mothers. And you see—" Half-guiltily she drew from her handsomely mounted black hand-bag a twist of crimson silk run through
by two fine knitting needles. "One never knows," she murmured.
"The new system has certainly given us a good deal of time to kill;
and sometimes I get tired just looking—even at this." Her gesture
was now addressed to the stupendous scene at their feet.

The dark lady laughed again, and they both relapsed upon the 7
view, contemplating it in silence, with a sort of diffused serenity
which might have been borrowed from the spring effulgence of the
Roman skies. The luncheon-hour was long past, and the two had
their end of the vast terrace to themselves. At its opposite extremity
a few groups, detained by a lingering look at the outspread city, were

gathering up guidebooks and fumbling for tips. The last of them scattered, and the two ladies were alone on the air-washed height.

"Well, I don't see why we shouldn't just stay here," said Mrs.   8
Slade, the lady of the high color and energetic brows. Two derelict basket-chairs stood near, and she pushed them into the angle of the parapet, and settled herself in one, her gaze upon the Palatine. "After all, it's still the most beautiful view in the world."

"It always will be, to me," assented her friend Mrs. Ansley, with   9
so slight a stress on the "me" that Mrs. Slade, though she noticed it, wondered if it were not merely accidental, like the random underlinings of old-fashioned letter-writers.

"Grace Ansley was always old-fashioned," she thought; and   10
added aloud, with a retrospective smile: "It's a view we've both been familiar with for a good many years. When we first met here we were younger than our girls are now. You remember?"

"Oh, yes, I remember," murmured Mrs. Ansley, with the same   11
undefinable stress—"There's that head-waiter wondering," she interpolated. She was evidently far less sure than her companion of herself and of her rights in the world.

"I'll cure him of wondering," said Mrs. Slade, stretching her   12
hand toward a bag as discreetly opulent-looking as Mrs. Ansley's. Signing to the head-waiter, she explained that she and her friend were old lovers of Rome, and would like to spend the end of the afternoon looking down on the view—that is, if it did not disturb the service? The head-waiter, bowing over her gratuity, assured her that the ladies were most welcome, and would be still more so if they would condescend to remain for dinner. A full moon night, they would remember.

Mrs. Slade's black brows drew together, as though references to   13
the moon were out-of-place and even unwelcome. But she smiled away her frown as the head-waiter retreated. "Well, why not? We might do worse. There's no knowing, I suppose, when the girls will be back. Do you even know back from *where? I* don't!"

Mrs. Ansley again colored slightly. "I think those young Italian   14
aviators we met at the Embassy invited them to fly to Tarquinia for tea. I suppose they'll want to wait and fly back by moonlight."

"Moonlight—moonlight! What a part it still plays. Do you sup-   15
pose they're as sentimental as we were?"

"I've come to the conclusion that I don't in the least know what   16
they are," said Mrs. Ansley. "And perhaps we didn't know much more about each other."

"No, perhaps we didn't."   17

Her friend gave her a shy glance. "I never should have supposed   18
you were sentimental, Alida."

"Well, perhaps I wasn't." Mrs. Slade drew her lids together in ret-   19
rospect; and for a few moments the two ladies, who had been intimate since childhood, reflected how little they knew each other. Each
one, of course, had a label ready to attach to the other's name; Mrs.
Delphin Slade, for instance, would have told herself, or any one who
asked her, that Mrs. Horace Ansley, twenty-five years ago, had been
exquisitely lovely—no, you wouldn't believe it, would you? . . .
though, of course, still charming, distinguished. . . . Well, as a girl she
had been exquisite; far more beautiful than her daughter Barbara,
though certainly Babs, according to the new standards at any rate,
was more effective—had more *edge*, as they say. Funny where she got
it, with those two nullities as parents. Yes; Horace Ansley was—well,
just the duplicate of his wife. Museum specimens of old New York.
Good-looking, irreproachable, exemplary. Mrs. Slade and Mrs.
Ansley had lived opposite each other—actually as well as figuratively—for years. When the drawing-room curtains in No. 20 East
73rd Street were renewed, No. 23, across the way, was always aware
of it. And of all the movings, buyings, travels, anniversaries, ill-
nesses—the tame chronicle of an estimable pair. Little of it escaped
Mrs. Slade. But she had grown bored with it by the time her husband
made his big *coup* in Wall Street, and when they bought in upper
Park Avenue had already begun to think: "I'd rather live opposite a
speak-easy for a change; at least one might see it raided." The idea of
seeing Grace raided was so amusing that (before the move) she
launched it at a woman's lunch. It made a hit, and went the rounds—
she sometimes wondered if it had crossed the street, and reached
Mrs. Ansley. She hoped not, but didn't much mind. Those were the
days when respectability was at a discount, and it did the irreproachable no harm to laugh at them a little.

A few years later, and not many months apart, both ladies lost   20
their husbands. There was an appropriate exchange of wreaths and
condolences, and a brief renewal of intimacy in the half-shadow of
their mourning; and now, after another interval, they had run across
each other in Rome, at the same hotel, each of them the modest
appendage of a salient daughter. The similarity of their lot had again
drawn them together, lending itself to mild jokes, and the mutual
confession that, if in old days it must have been tiring to "keep up"
with daughters, it was now, at times, a little dull not to.

No doubt, Mrs. Slade reflected, she felt her unemployment more 21
than poor Grace ever would. It was a big drop from being the wife of
Delphin Slade to being his widow. She had always regarded herself
(with a certain conjugal pride) as his equal in social gifts, as con-
tributing her full share to the making of the exceptional couple they
were: but the difference after his death was irremediable. As the wife
of the famous corporation lawyer, always with an international case
or two on hand, every day brought its exciting and unexpected obligation: the impromptu entertaining of eminent colleagues from
abroad, the hurried dashes on legal business to London, Paris or
Rome, where the entertaining was so handsomely reciprocated; the
amusement of hearing in her wake: "What, that handsome woman
with the good clothes and the eyes is Mrs. Slade—*the* Slade's wife?
Really? Generally the wives of celebrities are such frumps."

Yes; being *the* Slade's widow was a dullish business after that. In 22
living up to such a husband all her faculties had been engaged; now
she had only her daughter to live up to, for the son who seemed to
have inherited his father's gifts had died suddenly in boyhood. She
had fought through that agony because her husband was there, to be
helped and to help; now, after the father's death, the thought of the
boy had become unbearable. There was nothing left but to mother
her daughter; and dear Jenny was such a perfect daughter that she
needed no excessive mothering. "Now with Babs Ansley I don't
know that I should be so quiet," Mrs. Slade sometimes half-enviously
reflected; but Jenny, who was younger than her brilliant friend, was
that rare accident, an extremely pretty girl who somehow made
youth and prettiness seem as safe as their absence. It was all perplexing—and to Mrs. Slade a little boring. She wished that Jenny
would fall in love—with the wrong man, even; that she might have
to be watched, outmaneuvred, rescued. And instead, it was Jenny
who watched her mother, kept her out of draughts, made sure that
she had taken her tonic.

Mrs. Ansley was much less articulate than her friend, and her 23
mental portrait of Mrs. Slade was slighter, and drawn with fainter
touches. "Alida Slade's awfully brilliant; but not as brilliant as she
thinks," would have summed it up; though she would have added,
for the enlightenment of strangers, that Mrs. Slade had been an
extremely dashing girl; much more so than her daughter, who was
pretty, of course, and clever in a way, but had none of her mother's—
well, "vividness," someone had once called it. Mrs. Ansley would
take up current words like this, and cite them in quotation marks, as

unheard-of audacities. No: Jenny was not like her mother. Sometimes Mrs. Ansley thought Alida Slade was disappointed; on the whole she had had a sad life. Full of failures and mistakes; Mrs. Ansley had always been rather sorry for her. . . .

So these two ladies visualized each other, each through the 24 wrong end of her little telescope.

II

For a long time they continued to sit side by side without speak- 25 ing. It seemed as though, to both, there was a relief in laying down their somewhat futile activities in the presence of the vast Memento Mori which faced them. Mrs. Slade sat quite still, her eyes fixed on the golden slope of the Palace of the Caesars, and after a while Mrs. Ansley ceased to fidget with her bag, and she too sank into medita- tion. Like many intimate friends, the two ladies had never before had occasion to be silent together, and Mrs. Ansley was slightly embar- rassed by what seemed, after so many years, a new stage in their inti- macy, and one with which she did not yet know how to deal.

Suddenly the air was full of that deep clangor of bells which peri- 26 odically covers Rome with a roof of silver. Mrs. Slade glanced at her wristwatch. "Five o'clock already," she said, as though surprised.

Mrs. Ansley suggested interrogatively: "There's bridge at the 27 Embassy at five."

For a long time Mrs. Slade did not answer. She appeared to be 28 lost in contemplation, and Mrs. Ansley thought the remark had escaped her. But after a while she said, as if speaking out of a dream: "Bridge, did you say? Not unless you want to. . . . But I don't think I will, you know."

"Oh, no," Mrs. Ansley hastened to assure her. "I don't care to at 29 all. It's so lovely here; and so full of old memories, as you say." She settled herself in her chair, and almost furtively drew forth her knit- ting. Mrs. Slade took sideway note of this activity, but her own beau- tifully cared-for hands remained motionless on her knee.

"I was just thinking," she said slowly, "what different things 30 Rome stands for to each generation of travelers. To our grandmoth- ers, Roman fever; to our mothers, sentimental danger—how we used to be guarded!—to our daughters, no more dangers than the middle of Main Street. They don't know it—but how much they're missing!" The long golden light was beginning to pale, and Mrs. Ansley lifted her knitting a little closer to her eyes. "Yes; how we were guarded!"

"I always used to think," Mrs. Slade continued, "that our moth- 31
ers had a much more difficult job than our grandmothers. When
Roman fever stalked the streets it must have been comparatively
easy to gather in the girls at the danger hour; but when you and I
were young, with such beauty calling us, and the spice of disobedi-
ence thrown in, and no worse risk than catching cold during the cool
hour after sunset, the mothers used to be put to it to keep us in—
didn't they?"

She turned again toward Mrs. Ansley, but the latter had reached 32
a delicate point in her knitting. "One, two, three—slip two; yes, they
must have been," she assented, without looking up.

Mrs. Slade's eyes rested on her with a deepened attention. "She 33
can knit—in the face of *this*! How like her. . . ."

Mrs. Slade leaned back, brooding, her eyes ranging from the 34
ruins which faced her to the long green hollow of the Forum, the fading glow of the church fronts beyond it, and the outlying immensity
of the Colosseum. Suddenly she thought: "It's all very well to say
that our girls have done away with sentiment and moonlight. But if
Babs Ansley isn't out to catch that young aviator—the one who's a
Marchese—then I don't know anything. And Jenny has no chance
beside her. I know that too. I wonder if that's why Grace Ansley likes
the two girls to go everywhere together? My poor Jenny as a foil—!"
Mrs. Slade gave a hardly audible laugh, and at the sound Mrs.
Ansley dropped her knitting.

"Yes—?"   35

"I—oh, nothing. I was only thinking how your Babs carries 36
everything before her. That Campolieri boy is one of the best matches
in Rome. Don't look so innocent, my dear—you know he is. And I
was wondering, ever so respectfully, you understand, wondering
how two such exemplary characters as you and Horace had managed to produce anything quite so dynamic." Mrs. Slade laughed
again, with a touch of asperity.

Mrs. Ansley's hands lay inert across her needles. She looked 37
straight out at the great accumulated wreckage of passion and splendor at her feet. But her small profile was almost expressionless. At
length she said: "I think you overrate Babs, my dear."

Mrs. Slade's tone grew easier. "No; I don't. I appreciate her. And 38
perhaps envy you. Oh, my girl's perfect; if I were a chronic invalid
I'd—well, I think I'd rather be in Jenny's hands. There must be
times . . . but there! I always wanted a brilliant daughter . . . and
never quite understood why I got an angel instead."

Mrs. Ansley echoed her laugh in a faint murmur. "Babs is an 39 angel too."

"Of course—of course! But she's got rainbow wings. Well, 40 they're wandering by the sea with their young men; and here we sit . . . and it all brings back the past a little too acutely."

Mrs. Ansley had resumed her knitting. One might almost have 41 imagined (if one had known her less well, Mrs. Slade reflected) that, for her also, too many memories rose from the lengthening shadows of those august ruins. But no; she was simply absorbed in her work. What was there for her to worry about? She knew that Babs would almost certainly come back engaged to the extremely eligible Campolieri. "And she'll sell the New York house, and settle down near them in Rome, and never be in their way . . . she's much too tactful. But she'll have an excellent cook, and just the right people in for bridge and cocktails . . . and a perfectly peaceful old age among her grandchildren."

Mrs. Slade broke off this prophetic flight with a recoil of self- 42 disgust. There was no one of whom she had less right to think unkindly than of Grace Ansley. Would she never cure herself of envying her? Perhaps she had begun too long ago.

She stood up and leaned against the parapet, filling her troubled 43 eyes with the tranquilizing magic of the hour. But instead of tranquilizing her the sight seemed to increase her exasperation. Her gaze turned toward the Colosseum. Already its golden flank was drowned in purple shadow, and above it the sky curved crystal clear, without light or color. It was the moment when afternoon and evening hang balanced in mid-heaven.

Mrs. Slade turned back and laid her hand on her friend's arm. 44 The gesture was so abrupt that Mrs. Ansley looked up, startled.

"The sun's set. You're not afraid, my dear?"   45

"Afraid—?"   46

"Of Roman fever or pneumonia? I remember how ill you 47 were that winter. As a girl you had a very delicate throat, hadn't you?"

"Oh, we're all right up here. Down below, in the Forum, it does 48 get deathly cold, all of a sudden . . . but not here."

"Ah, of course you know because you had to be so careful." Mrs. 49 Slade turned back to the parapet. She thought: "I must make one more effort not to hate her." Aloud she said: "Whenever I look at the Forum from up here I remember that story about a great-aunt of yours, wasn't she? A dreadfully wicked great-aunt?"

"Oh yes; Great-aunt Harriet. The one who was supposed to have 50
sent her young sister out to the Forum after sunset to gather a night-
blooming flower for her album. All our great-aunts and grandmothers used to have albums of dried flowers."

Mrs. Slade nodded. "But she really sent her because they were in 51
love with the same man—"

"Well, that was the family tradition. They said Aunt Harriet con- 52
fessed it years afterward. At any rate, the poor little sister caught the
fever and died. Mother used to frighten us with the story when we
were children."

"And you frightened me with it, that winter when you and I 53
were here as girls. The winter I was engaged to Delphin."

Mrs. Ansley gave a faint laugh. "Oh, did I? Really frightened 54
you? I don't believe you're easily frightened."

"Not often; but I was then. I was easily frightened because I was 55
too happy. I wonder if you know what that means?"

"I—yes . . ." Mrs. Ansley faltered. 56

"Well, I suppose that was why the story of your wicked aunt 57
made such an impression on me. And I thought: 'There's no
more Roman fever, but the Forum is deathly cold after sunset—
especially after a hot day. And the Colosseum's even colder and
damper.'"

"The Colosseum—?" 58

"Yes. It wasn't easy to get in, after the gates were locked for the 59
night. Far from easy. Still, in those days it could be managed; it was
managed, often. Lovers met there who couldn't meet elsewhere. You
knew that?"

"I—I daresay. I don't remember." 60

"You don't remember? You don't remember going to visit some 61
ruins or other one evening, just after dark, and catching a bad chill?
You were supposed to have gone to see the moon rise. People always
said that expedition was what caused your illness."

There was a moment's silence; then Mrs. Ansley rejoined: "Did 62
they? It was all so long ago."

"Yes. And you got well again—so it didn't matter. But I suppose 63
it struck your friends—the reason given for your illness, I mean—
because everybody knew you were so prudent on account of your
throat, and your mother took such care of you. . . . You *had* been out
late sight-seeing, hadn't you, that night?"

"Perhaps I had. The most prudent girls aren't always prudent. 64
What made you think of it now?"

Mrs. Slade seemed to have no answer ready. But after a moment 65 she broke out: "Because I simply can't bear it any longer—!"

Mrs. Ansley lifted her head quickly. Her eyes were wide and 66 very pale. "Can't bear what?"

"Why—your not knowing that I've always known why you 67 went."

"Why I went—?" 68

"Yes. You think I'm bluffing, don't you? Well, you went to meet 69 the man I was engaged to—and I can repeat every word of the letter that took you there."

While Mrs. Slade spoke Mrs. Ansley had risen unsteadily to her 70 feet. Her bag, her knitting and gloves, slid in a panic-stricken heap to the ground. She looked at Mr. Slade as though she were looking at a ghost.

"No, no—don't," she faltered out. 71

"Why not? Listen, if you don't believe me. 'My one darling, 72 things can't go on like this. I must see you alone. Come to the Colosseum immediately after dark tomorrow. There will be somebody to let you in. No one whom you need fear will suspect'—but perhaps you've forgotten what the letter said?"

Mrs. Ansley met the challenge with an unexpected composure. 73 Steadying herself against the chair she looked at her friend, and replied: "No; I know it by heart too."

"And the signature? 'Only your D. S.' Was that it? I'm right, am 74 I? That was the letter that took you out that evening after dark?"

Mrs. Ansley was still looking at her. It seemed to Mrs. Slade that 75 a slow struggle was going on behind the voluntarily controlled mask of her small quiet face. "I shouldn't have thought she had herself so well in hand," Mrs. Slade reflected, almost resentfully. But at this moment Mrs. Ansley spoke, "I don't know how you knew. I burnt that letter at once."

"Yes; you would, naturally—you're so prudent!" The sneer was 76 open now. "And if you burnt the letter you're wondering how on earth I know what was in it. That's it, isn't it?"

Mrs. Slade waited, but Mrs. Ansley did not speak. 77

"Well, my dear, I know what was in that letter because I 78 wrote it!"

"You wrote it?" 79

"Yes." 80

The two women stood for a minute staring at each other in the 81 last golden light. Then Mrs. Ansley dropped back into her chair. "Oh," she murmured, and covered her face with her hands.

Mrs. Slade waited nervously for another word or movement. 82
None came, and at length she broke out: "I horrify you."

Mrs. Ansley's hands dropped to her knee. The face they uncov- 83
ered was streaked with tears. "I wasn't thinking of you. I was
thinking—it was the only letter I ever had from him!"

"And I wrote it. Yes; I wrote it! But I was the girl he was engaged 84
to. Did you happen to remember that?"

Mrs. Ansley's head drooped again. "I'm not trying to excuse 85
myself. . . . I remembered. . . ."

"And still you went?" 86

"Still I went." 87

Mrs. Slade stood looking down on the small bowed figure at her 88
side. The flame of her wrath had already sunk, and she wondered
why she had ever thought there would be any satisfaction in inflict-
ing so purposeless a wound on her friend. But she had to justify
herself.

"You do understand? I'd found out—and I hated you, hated you. 89
I knew you were in love with Delphin—and I was afraid; afraid of
you, of your quiet ways, your sweetness . . . your . . . well, I wanted
you out of the way, that's all. Just for a few weeks; just till I was sure
of him. So in a blind fury I wrote that letter. . . . I don't know why I'm
telling you now."

"I suppose," said Mrs. Ansley slowly, "it's because you've 90
always gone on hating me."

"Perhaps. Or because I wanted to get the whole thing off my 91
mind." She paused. "I'm glad you destroyed the letter. Of course I
never thought you'd die."

Mrs. Ansley relapsed into silence, and Mrs. Slade, leaning 92
above her, was conscious of a strange sense of isolation, of being cut
off from the warm current of human communion. "You think me a
monster!"

"I don't know. . . . It was the only letter I had, and you say he 93
didn't write it?"

"Ah, how you care for him still!" 94

"I cared for that memory," said Mrs. Ansley. 95

Mrs. Slade continued to look down on her. She seemed physi- 96
cally reduced by the blow—as if, when she got up, the wind might
scatter her like a puff of dust. Mrs. Slade's jealousy suddenly leapt up
again at the sight. All these years the woman had been living on that
letter. How she must have loved him, to treasure the mere memory
of its ashes! The letter of the man her friend was engaged to. Wasn't
it she who was the monster?

"You tried your best to get him away from me, didn't you? But 97 you failed; and I kept him. That's all."

"Yes. That's all." 98

"I wish now I hadn't told you. I'd no idea you'd feel about it as 99 you do; I thought you'd be amused. It all happened so long ago, as you say; and you must do me the justice to remember that I had no reason to think you'd ever taken it seriously. How could I, when you were married to Horace Ansley two months afterward? As soon as you could get out of bed your mother rushed you off to Florence and married you. People were rather surprised—they wondered at its being done so quickly; but I thought I knew. I had an idea you did it out of pique—to be able to say you'd got ahead of Delphin and me. Girls have such silly reasons for doing the most serious things. And your marrying so soon convinced me that you'd never really cared."

"Yes. I suppose it would," Mrs. Ansley assented. 100

The clear heaven overhead was emptied of all its gold. Dusk 101 spread over it, abruptly darkening the Seven Hills. Here and there lights began to twinkle through the foliage at their feet. Steps were coming and going on the deserted terrace—waiters looking out of the doorway at the head of the stairs, then reappearing with trays and napkins and flasks of wine. Tables were moved, chairs straightened. A feeble string of electric lights flickered out. Some vases of faded flowers were carried away, and brought back replenished. A stout lady in a dust-coat suddenly appeared, asking in broken Italian if any one had seen the elastic band which held together her tattered Baedeker. She poked with her stick under the table at which she had lunched, the waiters assisting.

The corner where Mrs. Slade and Mrs. Ansley sat was still shad- 102 owy and deserted. For a long time neither of them spoke. At length Mrs. Slade began again: "I suppose I did it as a sort of joke—"

"A joke?" 103

"Well, girls are ferocious sometimes, you know. Girls in love 104 especially. And I remember laughing to myself all that evening at the idea that you were waiting around there in the dark, dodging out of sight, listening for every sound, trying to get in.—Of course I was upset when I heard you were so ill afterward."

Mrs. Ansley had not moved for a long time. But now she turned 105 slowly toward her companion. "But I didn't wait. He'd arranged everything. He was there. We were let in at once," she said.

Mrs. Slade sprang up from her leaning position. "Delphin 106 there? They let you in?—Ah, now you're lying!" she burst out with violence.

Mrs. Ansley's voice grew clearer, and full of surprise. "But of   107
course he was there. Naturally he came—"

"Came? How did he know he'd find you there? You must be   108
raving!"

Mrs. Ansley hesitated, as though reflecting. "But I answered the   109
letter. I told him I'd be there. So he came."

Mrs. Slade flung her hands up to her face. "Oh, God—you   110
answered! I never thought of your answering. . . ."

"It's odd you never thought of it, if you wrote the letter."   111

"Yes. I was blind with rage."   112

Mrs. Ansley rose, and drew her fur scarf about her. "It is cold   113
here. We'd better go. I'm sorry for you," she said as she clasped the
fur about her throat.

The unexpected words sent a pang through Mrs. Slade. "Yes;   114
we'd better go." She gathered up her bag and cloak. "I don't know
why you should be sorry for me," she muttered.

Mrs. Ansley stood looking away from her toward the dusky   115
secret mass of the Colosseum. "Well—because I didn't have to wait
that night."

Mrs. Slade gave an unquiet laugh. "Yes; I was beaten there. But I   116
oughtn't to begrudge it to you, I suppose. At the end of all these
years. After all, I had everything; I had him for twenty-five years.
And you had nothing but that one letter that he didn't write."

Mrs. Ansley was again silent. At length she turned toward the   117
door of the terrace. She took a step, and turned back, facing her companion.

"I had Barbara," she said, and began to move ahead of Mrs.   118
Slade toward the stairway.

SOLDIER'S HOME

Ernest Hemingway

Krebs went to the war from a Methodist college in Kansas. There is a picture which shows him among his fraternity brothers, all of them wearing exactly the same height and style collar. He enlisted in the Marines in 1917 and did not return to the United States until the second division returned from the Rhine in the summer of 1919.

There is a picture which shows him on the Rhine with two German girls and another corporal. Krebs and the corporal look too big for their uniforms. The German girls are not beautiful. The Rhine does not show in the picture.

By the time Krebs returned to his home town in Oklahoma the greeting of heroes was over. He came back much too late. The men from the town who had been drafted had all been welcomed elaborately on their return. There had been a great deal of hysteria. Now the reaction had set in. People seemed to think it was rather ridiculous for Krebs to be getting back so late, years after the war was over.

At first Krebs, who had been at Belleau Wood, Soissons, the Champagne, St. Mihiel and in the Argonne did not want to talk about the war at all. Later he felt the need to talk but no one wanted to hear about it. His town had heard too many atrocity stories to be thrilled by actualities. Krebs found that to be listened to at all he had to lie, and after he had done this twice he, too, had a reaction against the war and against talking about it. A distaste for everything that had happened to him in the war set in because of the lies he had told. All of the times that had been able to make him feel cool and clean inside himself when he thought of them; the times so long back when he had done the one thing, the only thing for a man to do, easily and naturally, when he might have done something else, now lost their cool, valuable quality and then were lost themselves.

His lies were quite unimportant lies and consisted in attributing to himself things other men had seen, done or heard of, and stating as facts certain apocryphal incidents familiar to all soldiers. Even his lies were not sensational at the pool room. His acquaintances, who had heard detailed accounts of German women found chained to machine guns in the Argonne forest and who could not comprehend, or were barred by their patriotism from interest in, any German machine gunners who were not chained, were not thrilled by his stories.

Krebs acquired the nausea in regard to experience that is the 6
result of untruth or exaggeration, and when he occasionally met
another man who had really been a soldier and they talked a few
minutes in the dressing room at a dance he fell into the easy pose of
the old soldier among other soldiers: that he had been badly, sicken-
ingly frightened all the time. In this way he lost everything.

During this time, it was late summer, he was sleeping late in bed, 7
getting up to walk down town to the library to get a book, eating
lunch at home, reading on the front porch until he became bored and
then walking down through the town to spend the hottest hours of
the day in the cool dark of the pool room. He loved to play pool.

In the evening he practised on his clarinet, strolled down town, 8
read and went to bed. He was still a hero to his two young sisters.
His mother would have given him breakfast in bed if he had wanted
it. She often came in when he was in bed and asked him to tell her
about the war, but her attention always wandered. His father was
non-committal.

Before Krebs went away to the war he had never been allowed to 9
drive the family motor car. His father was in the real estate business
and always wanted the car to be at his command when he required
it to take clients out into the country to show them a piece of farm
property. The car always stood outside the First National Bank building where his father had an office on the second floor. Now, after the
war, it was still the same car.

Nothing was changed in the town except that the young girls 10
had grown up. But they lived in such a complicated world of already
defined alliances and shifting feuds that Krebs did not feel the energy
or the courage to break into it. He liked to look at them, though.
There were so many good-looking young girls. Most of them had
their hair cut short. When he went away only little girls wore their
hair like that or girls that were fast. They all wore sweaters and shirt
waists with round Dutch collars. It was a pattern. He liked to look at
them from the front porch as they walked on the other side of the
street. He liked to watch them walking under the shade of the trees.
He liked the round Dutch collars above their sweaters. He liked their
silk stockings and flat shoes. He liked their bobbed hair and the way
they walked.

When he was in town their appeal to him was not very strong. 11
He did not like them when he saw them in the Greek's ice cream parlor. He did not want them themselves really. They were too complicated. There was something else. Vaguely he wanted a girl but he did

not want to have to work to get her. He would have liked to have a girl but he did not want to have to spend a long time getting her. He did not want to get into the intrigue and the politics. He did not want to have to do any courting. He did not want to tell any more lies. It wasn't worth it.

He did not want any consequences. He did not want any conse- 12 quences ever again. He wanted to live along without consequences. Besides he did not really need a girl. The army had taught him that. It was all right to pose as though you had to have a girl. Nearly everybody did that. But it wasn't true. You did not need a girl. That was the funny thing. First a fellow boasted how girls mean nothing to him, that he never thought of them, that they could not touch him. Then a fellow boasted that he could not get along without girls, that he had to have them all the time, that he could not go to sleep without them.

That was all a lie. It was all a lie both ways. You did not need a 13 girl unless you thought about them. He learned that in the army. Then sooner or later you always got one. When you were really ripe for a girl you always got one. You did not have to think about it. Sooner or later it would come. He had learned that in the army.

Now he would have liked a girl if she had come to him and not 14 wanted to talk. But here at home it was all too complicated. He knew he could never get through it all again. It was not worth the trouble. That was the thing about French girls and German girls. There was not all this talking. You couldn't talk much and you did not need to talk. It was simple and you were friends. He thought about France and then he began to think about Germany. On the whole he had liked Germany better. He did not want to leave Germany. He did not want to come home. Still, he had come home. He sat on the front porch.

He liked the girls that were walking along the other side of the 15 street. He liked the look of them much better than the French girls or the German girls. But the world they were in was not the world he was in. He would like to have one of them. But it was not worth it. They were such a nice pattern. He liked the pattern. It was exciting. But he would not go through all the talking. He did not want one badly enough. He liked to look at them all, though. It was not worth it. Not now when things were getting good again.

He sat there on the porch reading a book on the war. It was a his- 16 tory and he was reading about all the engagements he had been in. It was the most interesting reading he had ever done. He wished there were more maps. He looked forward with a good feeling to reading all the really good histories when they would come out with good detail maps. Now he was really learning about the war. He had been a good soldier. That made a difference.

One morning after he had been home about a month his mother   17 came into his bedroom and sat on the bed. She smoothed her apron.

"I had a talk with your father last night, Harold," she said, "and   18 he is willing for you to take the car out in the evenings."

"Yeah?" said Krebs, who was not fully awake. "Take the car out?   19 Yeah?"

"Yes. Your father has felt for some time that you should be able   20 to take the car out in the evenings whenever you wished but we only talked it over last night."

"I'll bet you made him," Krebs said.   21

"No. It was your father's suggestion that we talk the matter   22 over."

"Yeah. I'll bet you made him," Krebs sat up in bed.   23

"Will you come down to breakfast, Harold?" his mother said.   24

"As soon as I get my clothes on," Krebs said.   25

His mother went out of the room and he could hear her frying   26 something downstairs while he washed, shaved and dressed to go down into the dining-room for breakfast. While he was eating breakfast his sister brought in the mail.

"Well, Hare," she said. "You old sleepy-head. What do you ever   27 get up for?"

Krebs looked at her. He liked her. She was his best sister.   28

"Have you got the paper?" he asked.   29

She handed him *The Kansas City Star* and he shucked off its   30 brown wrapper and opened it to the sporting page. He folded *The Star* open and propped it against the water pitcher with his cereal dish to steady it, so he could read while he ate.

"Harold," his mother stood in the kitchen doorway, "Harold,   31 please don't muss up the paper. You father can't read his *Star* if it's been mussed."

"I won't muss it," Krebs said.   32

His sister sat down at the table and watched him while he read.   33

"We're playing indoor[1] over at school this afternoon," she said.   34 "I'm going to pitch."

"Good," said Krebs. "How's the old wing?"   35

"I can pitch better than lots of the boys. I tell them all you taught   36 me. The other girls aren't much good."

"Yeah?" said Krebs.   37

---

[1] *indoor:* that is, a softball game played, of course, outdoors.

"I tell them all you're my beau. Aren't you my beau, Hare?" 38
"You bet." 39
"Couldn't your brother really be your beau just because he's 40
your brother?"
"I don't know." 41
"Sure you know. Couldn't you be my beau, Hare, if I was old 42
enough and if you wanted to?"
"Sure. You're my girl now." 43
"Am I really your girl?" 44
"Sure." 45
"Do you love me?" 46
"Uh, huh." 47
"Will you love me always?" 48
"Sure." 49
"Will you come over and watch me play indoor?" 50
"Maybe." 51
"Aw, Hare, you don't love me. If you loved me, you'd want to 52
come over and watch me play indoor."

Krebs's mother came into the dining-room from the kitchen. She 53
carried a plate with two fried eggs and some crisp bacon on it and a
plate of buckwheat cakes.

"You run along, Helen," she said. "I want to talk to Harold." 54

She put eggs and bacon down in front of him and brought in a 55
jug of maple syrup for the buckwheat cakes. Then she sat down
across the table from Krebs.

"I wish you'd put down the paper a minute. Harold," she said. 56
Krebs took down the paper and folded it. 57

"Have you decided what you are going to do yet, Harold?" his 58
mother said, taking off her glasses.

"No," said Krebs. 59

"Don't you think it's about time?" His mother did not say this in 60
a mean way. She seemed worried.

"I hadn't thought about it," Krebs said. 61

"God has some work for every one to do," his mother said. 62
"There can be no idle hands in His Kingdom."

"I'm not in His Kingdom," Krebs said. 63

"We are all of us in His Kingdom." 64

Krebs felt embarrassed and resentful as always. 65

"I've worried about you so much, Harold," his mother went on. 66
"I know the temptations you must have been exposed to. I know
how weak men are. I know what your own dear grandfather, my

own father, told us about the Civil War and I have prayed for you. I pray for you all day long, Harold."

Krebs looked at the bacon fat hardening on his plate. 67

"Your father is worried, too," his mother went on. "He thinks 68 you have lost your ambition, that you haven't got a definite aim in life. Charley Simmons, who is just your age, has a good job and is going to be married. The boys are all settling down; they're all determined to get somewhere; you can see that boys like Charley Simmons are on their way to being really a credit to the community."

Krebs said nothing. 69

"Don't look that way, Harold," his mother said. "You know we 70 love you and I want to tell you for your own good how matters stand. Your father does not want to hamper your freedom. He thinks you should be allowed to drive the car. If you want to take some of the nice girls out riding with you, we are only too pleased. We want you to enjoy yourself. But you are going to have to settle down to work, Harold. Your father doesn't care what you start in at. All work is honorable as he says. But you've got to make a start at something. He asked me to speak to you this morning and then you can stop in and see him at his office."

"Is that all?" Krebs said. 71

"Yes. Don't you love your mother, dear boy?" 72

"No," Krebs said. 73

His mother looked at him across the table. Her eyes were shiny. 74 She started crying.

"I don't love anybody," Krebs said. 75

It wasn't any good. He couldn't tell her, he couldn't make her see 76 it. It was silly to have said it. He had only hurt her. He went over and took hold of her arm. She was crying with her head in her hands.

"I didn't mean it," he said. "I was just angry at something. I 77 didn't mean I didn't love you."

His mother went on crying. Krebs put his arm on her shoulder. 78

"Can't you believe me, mother?" 79

His mother shook her head. 80

"Please, please, mother. Please believe me." 81

"All right," his mother said chokily. She looked up at him. "I 82 believe you, Harold."

Krebs kissed her hair. She put her face up to him. 83

"I'm your mother," she said. "I held you next to my heart when 84 you were a tiny baby."

Krebs felt sick and vaguely nauseated. 85

"I know, Mummy," he said. "I'll try and be a good boy for you." 86

"Would you kneel and pray with me, Harold?" his mother asked. 87

They knelt down beside the dining-room table and Krebs's 88
mother prayed.

"Now, you pray, Harold," she said. 89

"I can't," Krebs said. 90

"Try, Harold." 91

"I can't." 92

"Do you want me to pray for you?" 93

"Yes." 94

So his mother prayed for him and then they stood up and Krebs 95
kissed his mother and went out of the house. He had tried so to keep
his life from being complicated. Still, none of it had touched him. He
had felt sorry for his mother and she had made him lie. He would go
to Kansas City and get a job and she would feel all right about it.
There would be one more scene maybe before he got away. He would
not go down to his father's office. He would miss that one. He
wanted his life to go smoothly. It had just gotten going that way. Well,
that was all over now, anyway. He would go over to the schoolyard
and watch Helen play indoor baseball.

THE NECKLACE

Guy de Maupassant
Translated by Edgar V. Roberts

She was one of those pretty and charming women, born, as if by 1
an error of destiny, into a family of clerks and copyists. She had no
dowry, no prospects, no way of getting known, courted, loved, married by a rich and distinguished man. She finally settled for a marriage with a minor clerk in the Ministry of Education.

She was a simple person, without the money to dress well, but 2
she was as unhappy as if she had gone through bankruptcy, for
women have neither rank nor race. In place of high birth or important family connections, they can rely only on their beauty, their
grace, and their charm. Their inborn finesse, their elegant taste, their
engaging personalities, which are their only power, make working-
class women the equals of the grandest ladies.

She suffered constantly, feeling herself destined for all delicacies 3
and luxuries. She suffered because of her grim apartment with its
drab walls, threadbare furniture, ugly curtains. All such things,
which most other women in her situation would not even have
noticed, tortured her and filled her with despair. The sight of the
young country girl who did her simple housework awakened in her
only a sense of desolation and lost hopes. She daydreamed of large,
silent anterooms, decorated with oriental tapestries and lighted by
high bronze floor lamps, with two elegant valets in short culottes
dozing in large armchairs under the effects of forced-air heaters. She
imagined large drawing rooms draped in the most expensive silks,
with fine end tables on which were placed knickknacks of ines-
timable value. She dreamed of the perfume of dainty private rooms,
which were designed only for intimate tête-à-têtes with the closest
friends, who because of their achievements and fame would make
her the envy of all other women.

When she sat down to dinner at her round little table covered 4
with a cloth that had not been washed for three days, in front of her
husband who opened the kettle while declaring ecstatically, "Ah,
good old boiled beef! I don't know anything better," she dreamed of
expensive banquets with shining placesettings, and wall hangings
portraying ancient heroes and exotic birds in an enchanted forest.
She imagined a gourmet-prepared main course carried on the most

exquisite trays and served on the most beautiful dishes, with whispered gallantries which she would hear with a sphinxlike smile as she dined on the pink meat of a trout or the delicate wing of a quail.

She had no decent dresses, no jewels, nothing. And she loved 5 nothing but these; she believed herself born only for these. She burned with the desire to please, to be envied, to be attractive and sought after.

She had a rich friend, a comrade from convent days, whom she 6 did not want to see anymore because she suffered so much when she returned home. She would weep for the entire day afterward with sorrow, regret, despair, and misery.

Well, one evening, her husband came home glowing and carry- 7 ing a large envelope.

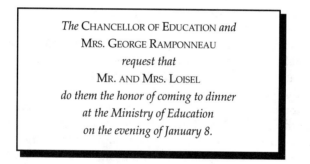

The Chancellor of Education *and*
Mrs. George Ramponneau
request that
Mr. and Mrs. Loisel
do them the honor of coming to dinner
at the Ministry of Education
on the evening of January 8.

"Here," he said, "this is something for you."   8

She quickly tore open the envelope and took out a card engraved 9 with these words:

Instead of being delighted, as her husband had hoped, she threw 10 the invitation spitefully on the table, muttering:

"What do you expect me to do with this?"   11

"But honey, I thought you'd be glad. You never get to go out, and 12 this is a special occasion! I had a lot of trouble getting the invitation. Everyone wants one. The demand is high and not many clerks get invited. Everyone important will be there."

She looked at him angrily and stated impatiently: 13

"What do you want me to wear to go there?"   14

He had not thought of that. He stammered: 15

"But your theater dress. That seems nice to me . . ."   16

He stopped, amazed and bewildered, as his wife began to cry. 17
Large tears fell slowly from the corners of her eyes to her mouth. He
said falteringly:

"What's wrong? What's the matter?"   18

But with a strong effort she had recovered, and she answered 19
calmly as she wiped her damp cheeks:

"Nothing, except that I have nothing to wear and therefore can't 20
go to the party. Give your invitation to someone else at the office
whose wife will have nicer clothes than mine."

Distressed, he responded: 21

"Well, all right, Mathilde. How much would a new dress cost, 22
something you could use at other times, but not anything fancy?"

She thought for a few moments, adding things up and thinking 23
also of an amount that she could ask without getting an immediate
refusal and a frightened outcry from the frugal clerk.

Finally she responded tentatively: 24

"I don't know exactly, but it seems to me that I could get by on 25
four hundred francs."

He blanched slightly at this, because he had set aside just that 26
amount to buy a shotgun for Sunday lark-hunts the next summer
with a few friends in the Plain of Nanterre.

However, he said: 27

"All right, you've got four hundred francs, but make it a pretty 28
dress."

As the day of the party drew near, Mrs. Loisel seemed sad, 29
uneasy, anxious, even though her gown was all ready. One evening
her husband said to her:

"What's the matter? You've been acting funny for several days." 30

She answered: 31

"It's awful, but I don't have any jewels to wear, not a single gem, 32
nothing to dress up my outfit. I'll look like a beggar. I'd almost rather
not go to the party."

He responded: 33

"You can wear a corsage of cut flowers. This year it's all the rage. 34
For only ten francs you can get two or three gorgeous roses."

She was not convinced.   35

"No . . . there's nothing more humiliating than looking shabby in 36
the company of rich women."

But her husband exclaimed: 37

"God, but you're silly! Go to your friend Mrs. Forrestier, and ask 38
her to lend you some jewelry. You know her well enough to do that."

She uttered a cry of joy: 39
"That's right. I hadn't thought of that." 40
The next day she went to her friend's house and described her 41
problem.
Mrs. Forrestier went to her mirrored wardrobe, took out a large 42
jewel box, opened it, and said to Mrs. Loisel:
"Choose, my dear." 43
She saw bracelets, then a pearl necklace, then a Venetian cross of 44
finely worked gold and gems. She tried on the jewelry in front of a
mirror, and hesitated, unable to make up her mind about each one.
She kept asking:
"Do you have anything else?" 45
"Certainly. Look to your heart's content. I don't know what 46
you'd like best."
Suddenly she found a superb diamond necklace in a black satin 47
box, and her heart throbbed with desire for it. Her hands shook as
she picked it up. She fastened it around her neck, watched it gleam
at her throat, and looked at herself ecstatically.
Then she asked, haltingly and anxiously: 48
"Could you lend me this, nothing but this?" 49
"Why yes, certainly." 50
She jumped up, hugged her friend joyfully, then hurried away 51
with her treasure.

The day of the party came. Mrs. Loisel was a success. She was 52
prettier than anyone else, stylish, graceful, smiling and wild with joy.
All the men saw her, asked her name, sought to be introduced. All
the important administrators stood in line to waltz with her. The
Chancellor himself eyed her.
She danced joyfully, passionately, intoxicated with pleasure, 53
thinking of nothing but the moment, in the triumph of her beauty, in
the glory of her success, on cloud nine with happiness made up of all
the admiration, of all the aroused desire, of this victory so complete
and so sweet to the heart of any woman.
She did not leave until four o'clock in the morning. Her husband, 54
since midnight, had been sleeping in a little empty room with three
other men whose wives had also been enjoying themselves.
He threw, over her shoulders, the shawl that he had brought for 55
the trip home—a modest everyday wrap, the poverty of which con-
trasted sharply with the elegance of her evening gown. She felt it and
hurried away to avoid being noticed by the other women who luxuriated in rich furs.
Loisel tried to hold her back: 56

"Wait a minute. You'll catch cold outdoors. I'll call a cab." 57

But she paid no attention and hurried down the stairs. When 58 they reached the street they found no carriages. They began to look for one, shouting at cabmen passing by at a distance.

They walked toward the Seine, desperate, shivering. Finally, on 59 a quay, they found one of those old night-going buggies that are seen in Paris only after dark, as if they were ashamed of their wretched appearance in daylight.

It took them to their door, on the Street of Martyrs, and they 60 sadly climbed the stairs to their flat. For her, it was finished. As for him, he could think only that he had to begin work at the Ministry of Education at ten o'clock.

She took the shawl off her shoulders, in front of the mirror, to see 61 herself once more in her glory. But suddenly she cried out. The necklace was no longer around her neck!

Her husband, already half undressed, asked: 62

"What's wrong?" 63

She turned toward him frantically: 64

"I . . . I . . . I no longer have Mrs. Forrestier's necklace." 65

He stood up, bewildered: 66

"What! . . . How! . . . It's not possible!" 67

And they looked in the folds of the gown, in the folds of the 68 shawl, in the pockets, everywhere. They found nothing.

He asked: 69

"You're sure you still had it when you left the party?" 70

"Yes. I checked it in the vestibule of the Ministry." 71

"But if you'd lost it in the street, we would've heard it fall. It 72 must be in the cab."

"Yes, probably. Did you notice the number?" 73

"No. Did you see it?" 74

"No." 75

Overwhelmed, they looked at each other. Finally, Loisel got 76 dressed again:

"I'm going out to retrace all our steps," he said, "to see if I can 77 find the necklace that way."

And he went out. She stayed in her evening dress, without the 78 energy to get ready for bed, stretched out in a chair, drained of strength and thought.

Her husband came back at about seven o'clock. He had found 79 nothing.

He went to Police Headquarters and to the newspapers to 80 announce a reward. He went to the small cab companies, and finally he followed up even the slightest hopeful lead.

She waited the entire day, in the same enervated state, in the face 81
of this frightful disaster.

Loisel came back in the evening, his face pale and haggard. He 82
had found nothing.

"You'll have to write to your friend," he said, "that you broke a 83
clasp on her necklace and that you're having it fixed. That'll give us
time to look around."

She wrote as he dictated. 84

By the end of the week they had lost all hope. 85

And Loisel, looking five years older, declared: 86

"We'll have to see about replacing the jewels." 87

The next day they took the case which had contained the neck- 88
lace and went to the jeweler whose name was inside. He looked at his
books:

"I wasn't the one, Madam, who sold the necklace. I only made 89
the case."

Then they went from jeweler to jeweler, searching for a necklace 90
like the other one, racking their memories, both of them sick with
worry and anguish.

In a shop in the Palais-Royal, they found a necklace of dia- 91
monds that seemed to them exactly like the one they were looking
for. It was priced at forty thousand francs. They could buy it for
thirty-six thousand.

They got the jeweler to promise not to sell it for three days. And 92
they made an agreement that he would buy it back for thirty-four
thousand francs if the original was recovered before the end of
February.

Loisel had saved eighteen thousand francs that his father had left 93
him. He would have to borrow the rest.

He borrowed, asking a thousand francs from one, five hundred 94
from another, five louis[1] here, three louis there. He wrote promissory
notes, undertook ruinous obligations, did business with finance companies and the whole tribe of loan sharks. He compromised himself
for the remainder of his days, risked his signature without knowing
whether he would be able to honor it; and, terrified by anguish over
the future, by the black misery that was about to descend on him, by
the prospect of all kinds of physical deprivations and moral tortures,

---

[1] *louis:* a gold coin worth twenty francs.

he went to get the new necklace, and put down thirty-six thousand francs on the jeweler's counter.

Mrs. Loisel took the necklace back to Mrs. Forrestier, who said 95 with an offended tone:

"You should have brought it back sooner; I might have 96 needed it."

She did not open the case, as her friend feared she might. If she 97 had noticed the substitution, what would she have thought? What would she have said? Would she not have taken her for a thief?

Mrs. Loisel soon discovered the horrible life of the needy. She did 98 her share, however, completely, heroically. That horrifying debt had to be paid. She would pay. They dismissed the maid; they changed their address; they rented an attic flat.

She learned to do the heavy housework, dirty kitchen jobs. She 99 washed the dishes, wearing away her manicured fingernails on greasy pots and encrusted baking dishes. She handwashed dirty linen, shirts, and dish towels that she hung out on the line to dry. Each morning, she took the garbage down to the street, and she carried up water, stopping at each floor to catch her breath. And, dressed in cheap house dresses, she went to the fruit dealer, the grocer, the butchers, with her basket under her arms, haggling, insulting, defending her measly cash penny by penny.

They had to make installment payments every month, and, to 100 buy more time, to refinance loans.

The husband worked evenings to make fair copies of trades- 101 men's accounts, and late into the night he made copies at five cents a page.

And this life lasted ten years. 102

At the end of ten years, they had paid back everything—every- 103 thing—including the extra charges imposed by loan sharks and the accumulation of compound interest.

Mrs. Loisel looked old now. She had become the strong, hard, 104 and rude woman of poor households. Her hair unkempt, with uneven skirts and rough, red hands, she spoke loudly, washed floors with large buckets of water. But sometimes, when her husband was at work, she sat down near the window, and she dreamed of that evening so long ago, of that party, where she had been so beautiful and so admired.

What would life have been like if she had not lost that necklace? Who knows? Who knows? Life is so peculiar, so uncertain. How little a thing it takes to destroy you or to save you!   105

Well, one Sunday, when she had gone for a stroll along the Champs-Elysées to relax from the cares of the week, she suddenly noticed a woman walking with a child. It was Mrs. Forrestier, still 106 youthful, still beautiful, still attractive.

Mrs. Loisel felt moved. Would she speak to her? Yes, certainly. And now that she had paid, she could tell all. Why not?

She walked closer.   107

"Hello, Jeanne."

The other gave no sign of recognition and was astonished to be 108 addressed so familiarly by this working-class woman. She stam- 109 mered: 110

"But . . . Madam! . . . I don't know. . . . You must have made a mistake."

"No. I'm Mathilde Loisel."   111

Her friend cried out:

"Oh! . . . My poor Mathilde, you've changed so much."   112

"Yes. I've had some tough times since I saw you last; in fact 113 hardships . . . and all because of you! . . ."   114

"Of me . . . how so?"   115

"You remember the diamond necklace that you lent me to go to the party at the Ministry of Education?"   116

"Yes. What then?"   117

"Well, I lost it."

"How, since you gave it back to me?"   118

"I returned another exactly like it. And for ten years we've been 119 paying for it. You understand this wasn't easy for us, who have noth- 120 ing. . . . Finally it's over, and I'm damned glad."   121

Mrs. Forrestier stopped her.

"You say that you bought a diamond necklace to replace mine?"

"Yes, you didn't notice it, eh? It was exactly like yours."   122

And she smiled with proud and childish joy.   123

Mrs. Forrestier, deeply moved, took both her hands.   124

"Oh, my poor Mathilde! But mine was only costume jewelry. At 125 most, it was worth only five hundred francs! . . ."   126

                127

ARABY

James Joyce

North Richmond Street,[1] being blind,[2] was a quiet street except at the hour when the Christian Brothers' School set the boys free. An uninhabited house of two storeys stood at the blind end, detached from its neighbours in a square ground. The other houses of the street, conscious of decent lives within them, gazed at one another with brown imperturbable faces.

The former tenant of our house, a priest, had died in the back drawing room. Air, musty from having long been enclosed, hung in all the rooms, and the waste room behind the kitchen was littered with old useless papers. Among these I found a few paper-covered books, the pages of which were curled and damp: *The Abbott*, by Walter Scott, *The Devout Communicant*[3] and *The Memoirs of Vidocq*.[4] I liked the last best because its leaves were yellow. The wild garden behind the house contained a central apple-tree and a few straggling bushes under one of which I found the late tenant's rusty bicycle-pump. He had been a very charitable priest; in his will he had left all his money to institutions and the furniture of his house to his sister.

When the short days of winter came dusk fell before we had well eaten our dinners. When we met in the street the houses had grown sombre. The space of sky above us was the colour of ever-changing violet and towards it the lamps of the street lifted their feeble lanterns. The cold air stung us and we played till our bodies glowed. Our shouts echoed in the silent street. The career of our play brought us through the dark muddy lanes behind the houses where we ran the gauntlet of the rough tribes from the cottages, to the back doors of the dark dripping gardens where odours arose from the ashpits, to the dark odorous stables where a coachman smoothed and combed the horse or shook music from the buckled harness. When we returned to the street light from the kitchen windows had filled the areas. If my uncle was seen turning the corner we hid in the shadow until we had seen him safely housed. Or if Mangan's sister came out

---

[1] *North Richmond Street:* name of a real street in Dublin on which Joyce lived as a boy.
[2] *blind:* dead-end street.
[3] *The Devout Communicant:* a book of meditations by Pacificus Baker, published 1873.
[4] *The Memoirs of Vidocq:* published 1829, the story of François Vidocq, a Parisian chief of detectives.

on the doorstep to call her brother in to his tea we watched her from our shadow peer up and down the street. We waited to see whether she would remain or go in and, if she remained, we left our shadow and walked up to Mangan's steps resignedly. She was waiting for us, her figure defined by the light from the half-opened door. Her brother always teased her before he obeyed and I stood by the railings looking at her. Her dress swung as she moved her body and the soft rope of her hair tossed from side to side.

Every morning I lay on the floor in the front parlor watching her 4 door. The blind was pulled down within an inch of the sash so that I could not be seen. When she came out on the doorstep my heart leaped. I ran to the hall, seized my books and followed her. I kept her brown figure always in my eye and, when we came near the point at which our ways diverged, I quickened my pace and passed her. This happened morning after morning. I had never spoken to her, except for a few casual words, and yet her name was like a summons to all my foolish blood.

Her image accompanied me even in places the most hostile to 5 romance. On Saturday evenings when my aunt went marketing I had to go to carry some of the parcels. We walked through the flaring street, jostled by drunken men and bargaining women, amid the curses of labourers, the shrill litanies of shop-boys who stood on guard by the barrels of pigs' cheeks, the nasal chanting of street singers, who sang a *come-all-you* about O'Donovan Rossa,[5] or a ballad about the troubles in our native land. These noises converged in a single sensation of life for me: I imagined that I bore my chalice safely through the throng of foes. Her name sprang to my lips at moments in strange prayers and praises which I myself did not understand. My eyes were often full of tears (I could not tell why) and at times a flood from my heart seemed to pour itself out into my bosom. I thought little of the future. I did not know whether I would ever speak to her or not or, if I spoke to her, how I could tell her of my confused adoration. But my body was like a harp and her words and gestures were like fingers running upon the wires.

One evening I went into the back drawing-room in which the 6 priest had died. It was a dark rainy evening and there was no sound in the house. Through one of the broken panes I heard the rain impinge upon the earth, the fine incessant needles of water playing in the sodden beds. Some distant lamp or lighted window gleamed

---

[5] *O'Donovan Rossa:* popular ballad about Jeremiah O'Donovan (1831–1915), a leader in the movement to free Ireland from English control. He was called "Dynamite Rossa."

below me. I was thankful that I could see so little. All my senses seemed to desire to veil themselves and, feeling that I was about to slip from them, I pressed the palms of my hands together until they trembled, murmuring: *O love! O love!* many times.

At last she spoke to me. When she addressed the first words to   7
me I was so confused that I did not know what to answer. She asked me was I going to *Araby*.[6] I forget whether I answered yes or no. It would be a splendid bazaar, she said; she would love to go.

—And why can't you? I asked.   8

While she spoke she turned a silver bracelet round and round   9
her wrist. She could not go, she said, because there would be a retreat[7] that week in her convent. Her brother and two other boys were fighting for their caps and I was alone at the railings. She held one of the spikes, bowing her head towards me. The light from the lamp opposite our-door caught the white curve of her neck, lit up her hair that rested there and, falling, lit up the hand upon the railing. It fell over one side of her dress and caught the white border of a petticoat, just visible as she stood at ease.

—It's well for you, she said.   10

—If I go, I said, I will bring you something.   11

What innumerable follies laid waste my waking and sleeping   12
thoughts after that evening! I wished to annihilate the tedious intervening days. I chafed against the work of school. At night in my bedroom and by day in the classroom her image came between me and the page I strove to read. The syllables of the word *Araby* were called to me through the silence in which my soul luxuriated and cast an Eastern enchantment over me. I asked for leave to go to the bazaar on Saturday night. My aunt was surprised and hoped it was not some Freemason[8] affair. I answered few questions in class. I watched my master's face pass from amiability to sternness; he hoped I was not beginning to idle. I could not call my wandering thoughts together. I had hardly any patience with the serious work of life which, now that it stood between me and my desire, seemed to me child's play, ugly monotonous child's play.

On Saturday morning I reminded my uncle that I wished to go   13
to the bazaar in the evening. He was fussing at the hall-stand, looking for the hatbrush, and answered me curtly:

—Yes, boy, I know.   14

---

[6] *Araby:* the bazaar held in Dublin from May 14–19, 1894.
[7] *retreat:* a special time set aside for concentrated religious instruction, discussion, and prayer.
[8] *Freemason:* and therefore Protestant.

As he was in the hall I could not go into the front parlour and lie 15
at the window. I left the house in bad humour and walked slowly
towards the school. The air was pitilessly raw and already my heart
misgave me.

When I came home to dinner my uncle had not yet been home. 16
Still, it was early. I sat staring at the clock for some time and, when its
ticking began to irritate me, I left the room. I mounted the staircase
and gained the upper part of the house. The high cold empty gloomy
rooms liberated me and I went from room to room singing. From the
front window I saw my companions playing below in the street.
Their cries reached me weakened and indistinct and, leaning my
forehead against the cool glass, I looked over at the dark house where
she lived. I may have stood there for an hour, seeing nothing but the
brown-clad figure cast by my imagination, touched discreetly by the
lamplight at the curved neck, at the hand upon the railing and at the
border below the dress.

When I came downstairs again I found Mrs. Mercer sitting at the 17
fire. She was an old garrulous woman, a pawnbroker's widow, who
collected used stamps for some pious purpose. I had to endure the
gossip of the tea-table. The meal was prolonged beyond an hour and
still my uncle did not come. Mrs. Mercer stood up to go: she was
sorry she couldn't wait any longer, but it was after eight o'clock and
she did not like to be out late, as the night air was bad for her. When
she had gone I began to walk up and down the room, clenching my
fists. My aunt said:

—I'm afraid you may put off your bazaar for this night of Our 18
Lord.

At nine o'clock I heard my uncle's latchkey in the halldoor. I 19
heard him talking to himself and heard the hall-stand rocking when
it had received the weight of his overcoat. I could interpret these
signs. When he was midway through his dinner I asked him to give
me the money to go to the bazaar. He had forgotten.

—The people are in bed and after their first sleep now, he said. 20

I did not smile. My aunt said to him energetically: 21

—Can't you give him the money and let him go? You've kept 22
him late enough as it is.

My uncle said he was very sorry he had forgotten. He said he 23
believed in the old saying: *All work and no play makes Jack a dull boy.*
He asked me where I was going and, when I had told him a second
time he asked me did I know *The Arab's Farewell to his Steed.*[9] When I

---
[9] *The Arab's Farewell to his Steed:* peom by Caroline Norton (1808–1877).

left the kitchen he was about to recite the opening lines of the piece to my aunt.

I held a florin[10] tightly in my hand as I strode down Buckingham 24
Street towards the station. The sight of the streets thronged with buyers and glaring with gas recalled to me the purpose of my journey. I took my seat in a third-class carriage of a deserted train. After an intolerable delay the train moved out of the station slowly. It crept onward among ruinous houses and over the twinkling river. At Westland Row Station a crowd of people pressed to the carriage doors; but the porters moved them back, saying that it was a special train for the bazaar. I remained alone in the bare carriage. In a few minutes the train drew up beside an improvised wooden platform. I passed out on to the road and saw by the lighted dial of a clock that it was ten minutes to ten. In front of me was a large building which displayed the magical name.

I could not find any sixpenny entrance and, fearing that the 25
bazaar would be closed, I passed in quickly through a turnstile, handing a shilling to a weary-looking man. I found myself in a big hall girdled at half its height by a gallery. Nearly all the stalls were closed and the greater part of the hall was in darkness. I recognized a silence like that which pervades a church after a service. I walked into the centre of the bazaar timidly. A few people were gathered about the stalls which were still open. Before a curtain, over which the words *Café Chantant* were written in coloured lamps, two men were counting money on a salver. I listened to the fall of the coins.

Remembering with difficulty why I had come I went over to one 26
of the stalls and examined porcelain vases and flowered tea-sets. At the door of the stall a young lady was talking and laughing with two young gentlemen. I remarked their English accents and listened vaguely to their conversation.

—O, I never said such a thing!   27
—O, but you did!   28
—O, but I didn't!   29
—Didn't she say that?   30
—Yes I heard her.   31
—O, there's a ... fib!   32

Observing me the young lady came over and asked me did I 33
wish to buy anything. The tone in her voice was not encouraging; she seemed to have spoken to me out of a sense of duty. I looked humbly

---

[10]*florin:* a two-shilling coin in the 1890s (when the story takes place), worth perhaps twenty dollars in today's money.

at the great jars that stood like eastern guards at either side of the dark entrance to the stall and murmured:

—No, thank you.   34

The young lady changed the position of one of the vases and 35 went back to the two young men. They began to talk of the same subject. Once or twice the young lady glanced at me over her shoulder.

I lingered before her stall, though I knew my stay was useless, to 36 make my interest in her wares seem the more real. Then I turned away slowly and walked down the middle of the bazaar. I allowed the two pennies to fall against the sixpence in my pocket. I heard a voice call from one end of the gallery that the light was out. The upper part of the hall was now completely dark.

Gazing up into the darkness I saw myself as a creature driven 37 and derided by vanity; and my eyes burned with anguish and anger.

YOUNG GOODMAN BROWN

Nathaniel Hawthorne

Young Goodman Brown came forth at sunset, into the street of 1
Salem village,[1] but put his head back, after crossing the threshold, to
exchange a parting kiss with his young wife. And Faith, as the wife
was aptly named, thrust her own pretty head into the street, letting
the wind play with the pink ribbons of her cap, while she called to
Goodman Brown.

"Dearest heart," whispered she, softly and rather sadly, when her 2
lips were close to his ear, "prithee, put off your journey until sunrise,
and sleep in your own bed tonight. A lone woman is troubled with
such dreams and such thoughts, that she's afeared of herself, sometimes. Pray, tarry with me this night, dear husband, of all nights in
the year!"

"My love and my Faith," replied young Goodman Brown, "of all 3
nights in the year, this one night must I tarry away from thee. My
journey, as thou callest it, forth and back again, must needs be done
'twixt now and sunrise. What, my sweet, pretty wife, dost thou
doubt me already, and we but three months married!"

"Then God bless you!" said Faith with the pink ribbons, "and 4
may you find all well, when you come back."

"Amen!" cried Goodman Brown. "Say thy prayers, dear Faith, 5
and go to bed at dusk, and no harm will come to thee."

So they parted; and the young man pursued his way, until, being 6
about to turn the corner by the meeting-house, he looked back and
saw the head of Faith still peeping after him, with a melancholy air,
in spite of her pink ribbons.

"Poor little Faith!" thought he, for his heart smote him. "What a 7
wretch am I, to leave her on such an errand! She talks of dreams, too.
Methought, as she spoke, there was trouble in her face, as if a dream
had warned her what work is to be done tonight. But no, no! 't would
kill her to think it. Well; she's a blessed angel on earth; and after this
one night, I'll cling to her skirts and follow her to Heaven."

With this excellent resolve for the future, Goodman Brown felt 8
himself justified in making more haste on his present evil purpose.
He had taken a dreary road, darkened by all the gloomiest trees of
the forest, which barely stood aside to let the narrow path creep

---

[1] *Salem village:* in Massachusetts, about fifteen miles north of Boston. The time of the story is the
late seventeenth or early eighteenth century.

through, and closed immediately behind. It was all as lonely as could be; and there is this peculiarity in such a solitude, that the traveller knows not who may be concealed by the innumerable trunks and the thick boughs overhead; so that, with lonely footsteps, he may yet be passing through an unseen multitude.

"There may be a devilish Indian behind every tree," said 9 Goodman Brown to himself; and he glanced fearfully behind him, as he added, "What if the devil himself should be at my very elbow!"

His head being turned back, he passed a crook of the road, and 10 looking forward again, beheld the figure of a man, in grave and decent attire, seated at the foot of an old tree. He arose at Goodman Brown's approach, and walked onward, side by side with him.

"You are late, Goodman Brown," said he. "The clock of the Old 11 South[2] was striking, as I came through Boston; and that is full fifteen minutes agone."

"Faith kept me back awhile," replied the young man, with a 12 tremor in his voice, caused by the sudden appearance of his companion, though not wholly unexpected.

It was now deep dusk in the forest, and deepest in that part of it 13 where these two were journeying. As nearly as could be discerned, the second traveller was about fifty years old, apparently in the same rank of life as Goodman Brown, and bearing a considerable resemblance to him, though perhaps more in expression than features. Still, they might have been taken for father and son. And yet, though the elder person was as simply clad as the younger, and as simple in manner too, he had an indescribable air of one who knew the world, and would not have felt abashed at the governor's dinner-table, or in King William's[3] court, were it possible that his affairs should call him thither. But the only thing about him that could be fixed upon as remarkable, was his staff, which bore the likeness of a great black snake, so curiously wrought, that it might almost be seen to twist and wriggle itself like a living serpent. This, of course, must have been an ocular deception, assisted by the uncertain light.

"Come, Goodman Brown!" cried his fellow-traveller, "this is a 14 dull pace for the beginning of a journey. Take my staff, if you are so soon weary."

"Friend," said the other, exchanging his slow pace for a full stop, 15 "having kept covenant by meeting thee here, it is my purpose now to

---

[2] *Old South:* The Old South Church, in Boston, is still there.
[3] *King William:* William III was kind of England from 1688 to 1701 (the time of the story). William IV was king from 1830 to 1837 (the period when Hawthorne wrote the story).

return whence I came. I have scruples, touching the matter thou wot'st of.[4]

"Sayest thou so?" replied he of the serpent, smiling apart. "Let us 16 walk on, nevertheless, reasoning as we go, and if I convince thee not, thou shalt turn back. We are but a little way in the forest, yet."

"Too far, too far!" exclaimed the goodman, unconsciously resum- 17 ing his walk. "My father never went into the woods on such an errand, nor his father before him. We have been a race of honest men and good Christians, since the days of the martyrs.[5] And shall I be the first of the name of Brown that ever took this path and kept—"

"Such company, thou wouldst say," observed the elder person, 18 interrupting his pause. "Well said, Goodman Brown! I have been as well acquainted with your family as ever a one among the Puritans; and that's no trifle to say. I helped your grandfather, the constable, when he lashed the Quaker woman so smartly through the streets of Salem. And it was I that brought your father a pitch-pine knot, kindled at my own hearth, to set fire to an Indian village, in King Philip's war.[6] They were my good friends, both; and many a pleasant walk have we had along this path, and returned merrily after midnight. I would fain be friends with you, for their sake."

"If it be as thou sayest," replied Goodman Brown, "I marvel they 19 never spoke of these matters. Or, verily, I marvel not, seeing that the least rumor of the sort would have driven them from New England. We are a people of prayer, and good works to boot, and abide no such wickedness."

"Wickedness or not," said the traveller with twisted staff, "I have 20 a very general acquaintance here in New England, The deacons of many a church have drunk the communion wine with me; the select-men, of divers towns, make me their chairman; and a majority of the Great and General Court are firm supporters of my interest. The governor and I, too—but these are state secrets."

"Can this be so!" cried Goodman Brown, with a stare of amaze- 21 ment at his undisturbed companion. "Howbeit, I have nothing to do with the governor and council; they have their own ways, and are no rule for a simple husbandman like me. But, were I to go on with thee, how should I meet the eye of that good old man, our minister, at

---

[4] *thou wot'st:* you know

[5] *days of the martyrs:* the martyrdoms of Protestants in England during the reign of Queen Mary (1553–1558).

[6] *King Philip's war:* This war (1675–1676), infamous for the atrocities committed by the New England settlers, resulted in the suppression of Indian tribal life and prepared the way for unlimited settlement of New England by European immigrants. "Philip" was the English name of Chief Metacomet of the Wampanoag tribe.

Salem village? Oh, his voice would make me tremble, both Sabbath-day and lecture-day!"

Thus far, the elder traveller had listened with due gravity, but   22
now burst into a fit of irrepressible mirth, shaking himself so violently, that his snakelike staff actually seemed to wriggle in sympathy.

"Ha! ha! ha!" shouted he, again and again; then composing him-   23
self, "Well, go on, Goodman Brown, go on; but, prithee, don't kill me with laughing!"

"Well, then, to end the matter at once," said Goodman Brown,   24
considerably nettled, "there is my wife, Faith. It would break her dear little heart; and I'd rather break my own!"

"Nay, if that be the case," answered the other, "e'en go thy ways,   25
Goodman Brown. I would not, for twenty old women like the one hobbling before us, that Faith should come to any harm."

As he spoke, he pointed his staff at a female figure on the path,   26
in whom Goodman Brown recognized a very pious and exemplary dame, who had taught him his catechism in youth, and was still his moral and spiritual adviser, jointly with the minister and Deacon Gookin.

"A marvel, truly, that Goody[7] Cloyse should be so far in the   27
wilderness, at nightfall!" said he. "But, with your leave, friend, I shall take a cut through the woods, until we have left this Christian woman behind. Being a stranger to you, she might ask whom I was consorting with, and whither I was going."

"Be it so," said his fellow-traveller. "Betake you to the woods,   28
and let me keep the path."

Accordingly, the young man turned aside, but took care to watch   29
his companion, who advanced softly along the road, until he had come within a staff's length of the old dame. She, meanwhile, was making the best of her way, with singular speed for so aged a woman, and mumbling some indistinct words, a prayer, doubtless, as she went. The traveller put forth his staff, and touched her with-ered neck with what seemed the serpent's tail.

"The devil!" screamed the pious old lady.   30

"Then Goody Cloyse knows her old friend?" observed the trav-   31
eller, confronting her, and leaning on his writhing stick.

"Ah, forsooth, and is it your worship, indeed?" cried the good   32
dame. "Yea, truly is it, and in the very image of my old gossip,[8]

---

[7] *Goody:* shortened form of "goodwife," a respectful name for a married woman of low rank. A "Goody Cloyse" was one of the women sentenced to execution by Hawthorne's great-grandfather, Judge John Hawthorne.

[8] *gossip:* from "good sib" or "good relative."

Goodman Brown, the grandfather of the silly fellow that now is. But, would your worship believe it? My broomstick hath strangely disappeared, stolen, as I suspect, by that unhanged witch, Goody Cory,[9] and that, too, when I was all anointed with the juice of smallage and cinquefoil and wolf's-bane—"[10]

"Mingled with fine wheat and the fat of a new-born babe," said   33 the shape of old Goodman Brown.

"Ah, your worship knows the recipe," cried the old lady, cack-   34 ling aloud. "So, as I was saying, being all ready for the meeting, and no horse to ride on, I made up my mind to foot it; for they tell me there is a nice young man to be taken into communion tonight. But now your good worship will lend me your arm, and we shall be there in a twinkling."

"That can hardly be," answered her friend. "I will not spare you   35 my arm, Goody Cloyse, but here is my staff, if you will."

So saying, he threw it down at her feet, where, perhaps, it   36 assumed life, being one of the rods which its owner had formerly lent to the Egyptian Magi.[11] Of this fact, however, Goodman Brown could not take cognizance. He had cast up his eyes in astonishment, and looking down again, beheld neither Goody Cloyse nor the serpentine staff, but his fellow-traveller alone, who waited for him as calmly as if nothing had happened.

"That old woman taught me my catechism!" said the young   37 man; and there was a world of meaning in this simple comment.

They continued to walk onward, while the elder traveller   38 exhorted his companion to make good speed and persevere in the path, discoursing so aptly, that his arguments seemed rather to spring up in the bosom of his auditor, than to be suggested by himself. As they went he plucked a branch of maple, to serve for a walking-stick, and began to strip it of the twigs and little boughs, which were wet with evening dew. The moment his fingers touched them, they became strangely withered and dried up, as with a week's sunshine. Thus the pair proceeded, at a good free pace, until suddenly, in a gloomy hollow of the road, Goodman Brown sat himself down on the stump of a tree, and refused to go any farther.

"Friend," said he, stubbornly, "my mind is made up. Not another   39 step will I budge on this errand. What if a wretched old woman do choose to go to the devil, when I thought she was going to Heaven! Is that any reason why I should quit my dear Faith, and go after her?"

---

[9] *Goody Cory:* name of a woman who was also sent to execution by Judge Hathorne.

[10] *smallage and cinquefoil and wolf's-bane:* plants commonly used by witches in making ointments.

[11] *lent to the Egyptian Magi:* See Exodus 7:10–12.

"You will think better of this by and by," said his acquaintance, 40
composedly. "Sit here and rest yourself a while; and when you feel
like moving again, there is my staff to help you along."

Without more words, he threw his companion the maple stick, 41
and was as speedily out of sight as if he had vanished into the deep-
ening gloom. The young man sat a few moments by the roadside,
applauding himself greatly, and thinking with how clear a conscience
he should meet the minister, in his morning walk, nor shrink from
the eye of good old Deacon Gookin. And what calm sleep would be
his, that very night, which was to have been spent so wickedly, but
purely and sweetly now, in the arms of Faith! Amidst these pleasant
and praiseworthy meditations, Goodman Brown heard the tramp of
horses along the road, and deemed it advisable to conceal himself
within the verge of the forest, conscious of the guilty purpose that
had brought him thither, though now so happily turned from it.

On came the hoof-tramps and the voices of the riders, two grave 42
old voices, conversing soberly as they drew near. These mingled
sounds appeared to pass along the road, within a few yards of the
young man's hiding-place; but owing, doubtless, to the depth of the
gloom, at that particular spot, neither the travellers nor their steeds
were visible. Though their figures brushed the small boughs by the
wayside, it could not be seen that they intercepted, even for a
moment, the faint gleam from the strip of bright sky, athwart which
they must have passed. Goodman Brown alternately crouched and
stood on tiptoe, pulling aside the branches, and thrusting forth his
head as far as he durst, without discerning so much as a shadow. It
vexed him the more, because he could have sworn, were such a thing
possible, that he recognized the voices of the minister and Deacon
Gookin, jogging[12] along quietly, as they were wont to do, when
bound to some ordination or ecclesiastical council. While yet within
hearing, one of the riders stopped to pluck a switch.

"Of the two, reverend Sir," said the voice like the deacon's, "I had 43
rather miss an ordination dinner than to-night's meeting. They tell
me that some of our community are to be here from Falmouth and
beyond, and others from Connecticut and Rhode Island; besides several of the Indian powwows,[13] who, after their fashion, know almost
as much deviltry as the best of us. Moreover, there is a goodly young
woman to be taken into communion."

---

[12]*jogging:* riding a horse at a slow trot.
[13]*powwow:* a Narragansett Indian word describing a priest or cult leader who led ritual cere-
monies of dance, incantation, and magic.

"Mighty well, Deacon Gookin!" replied the solemn old tones of   44
the minister. "Spur up, or we shall be late. Nothing can be done, you
know, until I get on the ground."

The hoofs clattered again, and the voices, talking so strangely in   45
the empty air, passed on through the forest, where no church had
ever been gathered, nor solitary Christian prayed. Whither, then,
could these holy men be journeying, so deep into the heathen wilderness? Young Goodman Brown caught hold of a tree, for support,
being ready to sink down on the ground, faint and over-burthened
with the heavy sickness of his heart. He looked up to the sky, doubt-
ing whether there really was a Heaven above him. Yet, there was the
blue arch, and the stars brightening in it.

"With Heaven above, and Faith below, I will yet stand firm   46
against the devil!" cried Goodman Brown.

While he still gazed upward, into the deep arch of the firmament,   47
and had lifted his hands to pray, a cloud, though no wind was stir-
ring, hurried across the zenith, and hid the brightening stars. The
blue sky was still visible, except directly overhead, where this black
mass of cloud was sweeping swiftly northward. Aloft in the air, as if
from the depths of the cloud, came a confused and doubtful sound of
voices. Once, the listener fancied that he could distinguish the
accents of town's people of his own, men and women, both pious
and ungodly, many of whom he had met at the communion-table,
and had seen others rioting at the tavern. The next moment, so indistinct were the sounds, he doubted whether he had heard aught but
the murmur of the old forest, whispering without a wind. Then came
a stronger swell of those familiar tones, heard daily in the sunshine,
at Salem village, but never, until now, from a cloud at night. There
was one voice, of a young woman, uttering lamentations, yet with an
uncertain sorrow, and entreating for some favor, which, perhaps, it
would grieve her to obtain. And all the unseen multitude, both saints
and sinners, seemed to encourage her onward.

"Faith!" shouted Goodman Brown, in a voice of agony and des-   48
peration; and the echoes of the forest mocked him, crying—"Faith!
Faith!" as if bewildered wretches were seeking her, all through the
wilderness.

The cry of grief, rage, and terror was yet piercing the night, when   49
the unhappy husband held his breath for a response. There was a
scream, drowned immediately in a louder murmur of voices fading
into far-off laughter, as the dark cloud swept away, leaving the clear
and silent sky above Goodman Brown. But something fluttered
lightly down through the air, and caught on the branch of a tree. The
young man seized it and beheld a pink ribbon.

"My Faith is gone!" cried he, after one stupefied moment. "There 50
is no good on earth, and sin is but a name. Come, devil! for to thee is
this world given."

And maddened with despair, so that he laughed loud and long, 51
did Goodman Brown grasp his staff and set forth again, at such a
rate, that he seemed to fly along the forest path, rather than to walk
or run. The road grew wilder and drearier, and more faintly traced,
and vanished at length, leaving him in the heart of the dark wilderness, still rushing onward, with the instinct that guides mortal man
to evil. The whole forest was peopled with frightful sounds; the
creaking of the trees, the howling of wild beasts, and the yell of
Indians; while, sometimes, the wind tolled like a distant church bell,
and sometimes gave a broad roar around the traveller, as if all Nature
were laughing him to scorn. But he was himself the chief horror of
the scene, and shrank not from its other horrors.

"Ha! ha! ha!" roared Goodman Brown, when the wind laughed 52
at him. "Let us hear which will laugh loudest! Think not to frighten
me with your deviltry! Come witch, come wizard, come Indian powwow, come devil himself! and here comes Goodman Brown. You may
as well fear him as he fear you!"

In truth, all through the haunted forest, there could be nothing 53
more frightful than the figure of Goodman Brown. On he flew,
among the black pines, brandishing his staff with frenzied gestures,
now giving vent to an inspiration of horrid blasphemy, and now
shouting forth such laughter, as set all the echoes of the forest laughing like demons around him. The fiend in his own shape is less
hideous than when he rages in the breast of man. Thus sped the
demoniac on his course, until, quivering among the trees, he saw a
red light before him, as when the felled trunks and branches of a
clearing have been set on fire, and throw up their lurid blaze against
the sky, at the hour of midnight. He paused, in a lull of the tempest
that had driven him onward, and heard the swell of what seemed a
hymn, rolling solemnly from a distance, with the weight of many
voices. He knew the tune. It was a familiar one in the choir of the village meeting-house. The verse died heavily away, and was length-
ened by a chorus, not of human voices, but of all the sounds of the
benighted wilderness, pealing in awful harmony together. Goodman
Brown cried out; and his cry was lost to his own ear, by its unison
with the cry of the desert.

In the interval of silence, he stole forward, until the light glared 54
full upon his eyes. At one extremity of an open space, hemmed in by
the dark wall of the forest, arose a rock, bearing some rude, natural

resemblance either to an altar or a pulpit, and surrounded by four blazing pines, their tops aflame, their stems untouched, like candles at an evening meeting. The mass of foliage, that had overgrown the summit of the rock, was all on fire, blazing high into the night, and fitfully illuminating the whole field. Each pendent twig and leafy festoon was in a blaze. As the red light arose and fell, a numerous congregation alternately shone forth, then disappeared in shadow, and again grew, as it were, out of the darkness, peopling the heart of the solitary woods at once.

"A grave and dark-clad company!" quoth Goodman Brown.   55

In truth, they were such. Among them, quivering to-and-fro, 56 between gloom and splendor, appeared faces that would be seen, next day, at the council-board of the province, and others which, Sabbath after Sabbath, looked devoutly heavenward, and benignantly over the crowded pews, from the holiest pulpits in the land. Some affirm that the lady of the governor was there. At least, there were high dames well known to her, and wives of honored husbands, and widows a great multitude, and ancient maidens, all of excellent repute, and fair young girls, who trembled lest their mothers should espy them. Either the sudden gleams of light, flashing over the obscure field, bedazzled Goodman Brown, or he recognized a score of the church members of Salem village, famous for their especial sanctity. Good old Deacon Gookin had arrived, and waited at the skirts of that venerable saint, his reverend pastor. But, irreverently consorting with these grave, reputable, and pious people, these elders of the church, these chaste dames and dewy virgins, there were men of dissolute lives and women of spotted fame, wretches given over to all mean and filthy vice, and suspected even of horrid crimes. It was strange to see, that the good shrank not from the wicked, nor were the sinners abashed by the saints. Scattered, also, among their pale-faced enemies, were the Indian priests, or powwows, who had often scared their native forest with more hideous incantations than any known to English witchcraft.

"But, where is Faith?" thought Goodman Brown; and, as hope 57 came into his heart, he trembled.

Another verse of the hymn arose, a slow and mournful strain, 58 such as the pious love, but joined to words which expressed all that our nature can conceive of sin, and darkly hinted at far more. Unfathomable to mere mortals is the lore of fiends. Verse after verse was sung, and still the chorus of the desert swelled between, like the deepest tone of a mighty organ. And, with the final peal of that dreadful anthem, there came a sound, as if the roaring wind, the rushing streams, the howling beasts, and every other voice of the unconverted wilderness were mingling and according with the voice of guilty man, in homage to the prince of all. The four blazing pines threw up a loftier flame, and obscurely discovered shapes and visages of horror on the smoke-wreaths, above the impious assembly. At the same moment, the fire on the rock shot redly forth, and formed a glowing arch above its base, where now appeared a figure. With reverence be it spoken, the apparition bore no slight similitude, both in garb and manner, to some grave divine of the New England churches.

"Bring forth the converts!" cried a voice, that echoed through the 59 field and rolled into the forest.

At the word, Goodman Brown stepped forth from the shadow of 60 the trees, and approached the congregation, with whom he felt a loathful brotherhood, by the sympathy of all that was wicked in his heart. He could have well-nigh sworn, that the shape of his own dead father beckoned him to advance, looking downward from a smoke-wreath, while a woman, with dim features of despair, threw out her hand to warn him back. Was it his mother? But he had no power to retreat one step, nor to resist, even in thought, when the minister and good old Deacon Gookin seized his arms, and led him to the blazing rock. Thither came also the slender form of a veiled female, led between Goody Cloyse, that pious teacher of the catechism, and Martha Carrier, who had received the devil's promise to be queen of hell. A rampant hag was she! And there stood the proselytes, beneath the canopy of fire.

"Welcome, my children," said the dark figure, "to the commu- 61 nion of your race! Ye have found, thus young, your nature and your destiny. My children, look behind you!"

They turned; and flashing forth, as it were, in a sheet of flame, the 62 fiend-worshippers were seen; the smile of welcome gleamed darkly on every visage.

"There," resumed the sable form, "are all whom ye have rever- 63 enced from youth. Ye deemed them holier than yourselves, and shrank from your own sin, contrasting it with their lives of righteousness and prayerful aspirations heavenward. Yet, here are they all, in my worshipping assembly! This night it shall be granted you to know their secret deeds; how hoary-bearded elders of the church have whispered wanton words to the young maids of their households; how many a woman, eager for widow's weeds, has given her husband a drink at bedtime, and let him sleep his last sleep in her bosom; how beardless youths have made haste to inherit their father's wealth; and how fair damsels—blush not, sweet ones!—have dug little graves in the garden, and bidden me, the sole guest, to an infant's funeral. By the sympathy of your human hearts for sin, ye shall scent out all the places—whether in church, bed-chamber, street, field, or forest—where crime has been committed, and shall exult to behold the whole earth one stain of guilt, one mighty blood-spot. Far more than this! It shall be yours to penetrate, in every bosom, the deep mystery of sin, the fountain of all wicked arts, and which inexhaustibly supplies more evil impulses than human power—than my power, at its utmost!—can make manifest in deeds. And now, my children, look upon each other."

They did so; and, by the blaze of the hell-kindled torches, the 64 wretched man beheld his Faith, and the wife her husband, trembling before that unhallowed altar.

"Lo! there ye stand, my children," said the figure, in a deep and 65 solemn tone, almost sad, with its despairing awfulness, as if his once angelic nature[14] could yet mourn for our miserable race. "Depending upon one another's hearts, ye had still hoped that virtue were not all a dream! Now are ye undeceived!—Evil is the nature of mankind. Evil must be your only happiness. Welcome, again, my children, to the communion of your race!"

"Welcome!" repeated the fiend-worshippers, in one cry of 66 despair and triumph.

And there they stood, the only pair, as it seemed, who were yet 67 hesitating on the verge of wickedness, in this dark world. A basin was hollowed, naturally, in the rock. Did it contain water, reddened by the lurid light? or was it blood? or, perchance, a liquid flame? Herein did the Shape of Evil dip his hand, and prepare to lay the mark of baptism upon their foreheads, that they might be partakers of the mystery of sin, more conscious of the secret guilt of others, both in deed and thought, than they could now be of their own. The husband cast one look at his pale wife, and Faith at him. What pol-luted wretches would the next glance show them to each other, shud-dering alike at what they disclosed and what they saw!

"Faith! Faith!" cried the husband. "Look up to Heaven, and resist 68 the Wicked One!"

Whether Faith obeyed, he knew not. Hardly had he spoken, 69 when he found himself amid calm night and solitude, listening to a roar of the wind, which died heavily away through the forest. He

---

[14]*once angelic nature:* Lucifer ("light bearer"), another name for the Devil, led the traditional revolt of the angels and was thrown into hell as his punishment. See Isaiah 14:12–**15**.

staggered against the rock, and felt it chill and damp, while a hanging twig, that had been all on fire, besprinkled his cheek with the
coldest dew.

The next morning, young Goodman Brown came slowly into the   70
street of Salem village staring around him like a bewildered man. The
good old minister was taking a walk along the grave-yard, to get an
appetite for breakfast and meditate his sermon, and bestowed a
blessing, as he passed, on Goodman Brown. He shrank from the venerable saint, as if to avoid an anathema. Old Deacon Gookin was at
domestic worship, and the holy words of his prayer were heard
through the open window. "What God doth the wizard pray to?"
quoth Goodman Brown. Goody Cloyse, that excellent old Christian,
stood in the early sunshine, at her own lattice, catechising a little
girl, who had brought her a pint of morning's milk. Goodman
Brown snatched away the child, as from the grasp of the fiend himself. Turning the corner by the meetinghouse, he spied the head of
Faith, with the pink ribbons, gazing anxiously forth, and bursting
into such joy at the sight of him that she skipt along the street, and
almost kissed her husband before the whole village. But Goodman
Brown looked sternly and sadly into her face, and passed on without
a greeting.

Had Goodman Brown fallen asleep in the forest, and only   71
dreamed a wild dream of a witch-meeting?

Be it so, if you will. But, alas! it was a dream of evil omen for   72
young Goodman Brown. A stern, a sad, a darkly meditative, a dis-
trustful, if not a desperate man did he become, from the night of that
fearful dream. On the Sabbath day, when the congregation were
singing a holy psalm, he could not listen, because an anthem of sin
rushed loudly upon his ear, and drowned all the blessed strain.
When the minister spoke from the pulpit, with power and fervid elo-
quence, and with his hand on the open Bible, of the sacred truths of
our religion, and of saint-like lives and triumphant deaths, and of
future bliss or misery unutterable, then did Goodman Brown turn
pale, dreading lest the roof should thunder down upon the gray blas-
phemer and his hearers. Often, awaking suddenly at midnight, he
shrank from the bosom of Faith, and at morning or eventide, when
the family knelt down in prayer, he scowled, and muttered to himself, and gazed sternly at his wife, and turned away. And when he
had lived long, and was borne to his grave, a hoary corpse, followed
by Faith, an aged woman, and children and grandchildren, a goodly
procession, besides neighbors not a few, they carved no hopeful
verse upon his tombstone; for his dying hour was gloom.

THE STORY OF AN HOUR

Kate Chopin

Knowing that Mrs. Mallard was afflicted with a heart trouble, 1
great care was taken to break to her as gently as possible the news of
her husband's death.

It was her sister Josephine who told her, in broken sentences: 2
veiled hints that revealed in half concealing. Her husband's friend
Richards was there, too, near her. It was he who had been in the
newspaper office when intelligence of the railroad disaster was
received, with Brently Mallard's name leading the list of "killed." He
had only taken the time to assure himself of its truth by a second
telegram, and had hastened to forestall any less careful, less tender
friend in bearing the sad message.

She did not hear the story as many women have heard the same, 3
with a paralyzed inability to accept its significance. She wept at once,
with sudden, wild abandonment, in her sister's arms. When the
storm of grief had spent itself she went away to her room alone. She
would have no one follow her.

There stood, facing the open window, a comfortable, roomy arm- 4
chair. Into this she sank, pressed down by a physical exhaustion that
haunted her body and seemed to reach into her soul.

She could see in the open square before her house the tops of 5
trees that were all aquiver with the new spring life. The delicious
breath of rain was in the air. In the street below a peddler was crying
his wares. The notes of a distant song which some one was singing
reached her faintly, and countless sparrows were twittering in the
eaves.

There were patches of blue sky showing here and there through 6
the clouds that had met and piled one above the other in the west facing her window.

She sat with her head thrown back upon the cushion of the chair, 7
quite motionless, except when a sob came up into her throat and
shook her, as a child who has cried itself to sleep continues to sob in
its dreams.

She was young, with a fair, calm face, whose lines bespoke 8
repression and even a certain strength. But now there was a dull stare
in her eyes, whose gaze was fixed away off yonder on one of those
patches of blue sky. It was not a glance of reflection, but rather indi-
cated a suspension of intelligent thought.

There was something coming to her and she was waiting for it, 9
fearfully. What was it? She did not know; it was too subtle and elu-
sive to name. But she felt it, creeping out of the sky, reaching toward
her through the sounds, the scents, the color that filled the air.

Now her bosom rose and fell tumultuously. She was beginning 10
to recognize this thing that was approaching to possess her, and she
was striving to beat it back with her will—as powerless as her two
white slender hands would have been.

When she abandoned herself a little whispered word escaped 11
her slightly parted lips. She said it over and over under her breath:
"free, free, free!" The vacant stare and the look of terror that had followed it went from her eyes. They stayed keen and bright. Her pulses
beat fast, and the coursing blood warmed and relaxed every inch of
her body.

She did not stop to ask if it were or were not a monstrous joy that 12
held her. A clear and exalted perception enabled her to dismiss the
suggestion as trivial.

She knew that she would weep again when she saw the kind, 13
tender hands folded in death; the face that had never looked save
with love upon her, fixed and gray and dead. But she saw beyond
that bitter moment a long procession of years to come that would
belong to her absolutely. And she opened and spread her arms out to
them in welcome.

There would be no one to live for during those coming years; she 14
would live for herself. There would be no powerful will bending hers
in that blind persistence with which men and women believe they
have a right to impose a private will upon a fellow-creature. A kind
intention or a cruel intention made the act seem no less a crime as she
looked upon it in that brief moment of illumination.

And yet she had loved him—sometimes. Often she had not. 15
What did it matter! What could love, the unsolved mystery, count for
in face of this possession of self-assertion which she suddenly recognized as the strongest impulse of her being!

"Free! Body and soul free!" she kept whispering. 16

Josephine was kneeling before the closed door with her lips to 17
the keyhole, imploring for admission. "Louise, open the door! I beg;
open the door—you will make yourself ill. What are you doing,
Louise? For heaven's sake open the door."

"Go away. I am not making myself ill." No; she was drinking in 18
a very elixir of life through that open window.

Her fancy was running riot along those days ahead of her. Spring 19
days, and summer days, and all sorts of days that would be her own.

She breathed a quick prayer that life might be long. It was only yesterday she had thought with a shudder that life might be long.

She arose at length and opened the door to her sister's importunities. There was a feverish triumph in her eyes, and she carried herself unwittingly like a goddess of Victory. She clasped her sister's waist, and together they descended the stairs. Richards stood waiting for them at the bottom. 20

Some one was opening the front door with a latchkey. It was Brently Mallard who entered, a little travel-stained, composedly carrying his grip-sack and umbrella. He had been far from the scene of accident, and did not even know there had been one. He stood amazed at Josephine's piercing cry: at Richards' quick motion to screen him from the view of his wife. 21

But Richards was too late. 22

When the doctors came they said she had died of heart disease— of joy that kills. 23

THE YELLOW WALLPAPER[1]

Charlotte Perkins Gilman

It is very seldom that mere ordinary people like John and myself 1
secure ancestral halls for the summer.

A colonial mansion, a hereditary estate, I would say a haunted 2
house and reach the height of romantic felicity—but that would be
asking too much of fate!

Still I will proudly declare that there is something queer about it. 3

Else, why should it be let so cheaply? And why have stood so 4
long untenanted?

John laughs at me, of course, but one expects that. 5

John is practical in the extreme. He has no patience with faith, an 6
intense horror of superstition, and he scoffs openly at any talk of
things not to be felt and seen and put down in figures.

John is a physician, and *perhaps*—(I would not say it to a living 7
soul, of course, but this is dead paper and a great relief to my
mind)—*perhaps* that is one reason I do not get well faster.

You see, he does not believe I am sick! And what can one do? 8

If a physician of high standing, and one's own husband, assures 9
friends and relatives that there is really nothing the matter with one
but temporary nervous depression—a slight hysterical tendency—
what is one to do?

My brother is also a physician, and also of high standing, and he 10
says the same thing.

So I take phosphates or phosphites—whichever it is—and tonics, 11
and air and exercise, and journeys, and am absolutely forbidden to
"work" until I am well again.

Personally, I disagree with their ideas. 12

Personally, I believe that congenial work, with excitement and 13
change, would do me good.

But what is one to do? 14

---

[1] *The Yellow Wallpaper:* The story is based on the "rest cure" developed after the Civil War by the famous Philadelphia physician S. Weir Mitchell (1829–1914); see paragraph 83. The Mitchell treatment required confining the patient to a hospital, hotel, or some other remote residence. Once isolated, the patient was to have complete bed rest, increased food intake, iron supplements, exercise, and sometimes massage and electric shock therapy. Gilman had experienced Mitchell's "cure," and sent a copy of this story to him as criticism. After receiving the story Mitchell modified his methods..

I did write for a while in spite of them; but it *does* exhaust me a 15 good deal—having to be so sly about it, or else meet with heavy opposition.

I sometimes fancy that in my condition, if I had less opposition 16 and more society and stimulus—but John says the very worst thing I can do is to think about my condition, and I confess it always makes me feel bad.

So I will let it alone and talk about the house. 17

The most beautiful place! It is quite alone, standing well back 18 from the road, quite three miles from the village. It makes me think of English places that you read about, for there are hedges and walls and gates that lock, and lots of separate little houses for the gardeners and people.

There is a *delicious* garden! I never saw such a garden—large and 19 shady, full of box-bordered paths, and lined with long grape-covered arbors with seats under them.

There were greenhouses, but they are all broken now. 20

There was some legal trouble, I believe, something about the 21 heirs and co-heirs; anyhow, the place has been empty for years.

That spoils my ghostliness, I am afraid, but I don't care—there is 22 something strange about the house—I can feel it.

I even said so to John one moonlight evening, but he said what I 23 felt was a draught, and shut the window.

I get unreasonably angry with John sometimes. I'm sure I never 24 used to be so sensitive. I think it is due to this nervous condition.

But John says if I feel so I shall neglect proper self-control; so I 25 take pains to control myself—before him, at least, and that makes me very tired.

I don't like our room a bit. I wanted one downstairs that opened 26 onto the piazza and had roses all over the window, and such pretty old-fashioned chintz hangings! But John would not hear of it.

He said there was only one window and not room for two beds, 27 and no near room for him if he took another.

He is very careful and loving, and hardly lets me stir without 28 special direction.

I have a schedule prescription for each hour in the day; he takes 29 all care from me, and so I feel basely ungrateful not to value it more.

He said he came here solely on my account, that I was to have 30 perfect rest and all the air I could get. "Your exercise depends on your strength, my dear," said he, "and your food somewhat on your appetite; but air you can absorb all the time." So we took the nursery at the top of the house.

It is a big, airy room, the whole floor nearly, with windows that 31 look all ways, and air and sunshine galore. It was nursery first, and then playroom and gymnasium, I should judge, for the windows are barred for little children, and there are rings and things in the walls.

The paint and paper look as if a boys' school had used it. It is 32 stripped off—the paper—in great patches all around the head of my bed, about as far as I can reach, and in a great place on the other side of the room low down. I never saw a worse paper in my life. One of those sprawling, flamboyant patterns committing every artistic sin.

It is dull enough to confuse the eye in following, pronounced 33 enough constantly to irritate and provoke study, and when you follow the lame uncertain curves for a little distance they suddenly commit suicide—plunge off at outrageous angles, destroy themselves in unheard-of contradictions.

The color is repellent, almost revolting: a smouldering unclean 34 yellow, strangely faded by the slow-turning sunlight. It is a dull yet lurid orange in some places, a sickly sulphur tint in others.

No wonder the children hated it! I should hate it myself if I had 35 to live in this room long.

There comes John, and I must put this away—he hates to have 36 me write a word.

We have been here two weeks, and I haven't felt like writing 37 before, since that first day.

I am sitting by the window now, up in this atrocious nursery, and 38 there is nothing to hinder my writing as much as I please, save lack of strength.

John is away all day, and even some nights when his cases are 39 serious.

I am glad my case is not serious! 40

But these nervous troubles are dreadfully depressing. 41

John does not know how much I really suffer. He knows there is 42 no reason to suffer, and that satisfies him.

Of course it is only nervousness. It does weigh on me so not to 43 do my duty in any way!

I meant to be such a help to John, such a real rest and comfort, 44 and here I am a comparative burden already!

Nobody would believe what an effort it is to do what little I am 45 able—to dress and entertain, and order things.

It is fortunate Mary is so good with the baby. Such a dear baby! 46

And yet I *cannot* be with him, it makes me so nervous. 47

I suppose John never was nervous in his life. He laughs at me so 48
about this wallpaper!

At first he meant to repaper the room, but afterward he said that 49
I was letting it get the better of me, and that nothing was worse for a
nervous patient than to give way to such fancies.

He said that after the wallpaper was changed it would be the 50
heavy bedstead, and then the barred windows, and then that gate at
the head of the stairs, and so on.

"You know the place is doing you good," he said, "and really, 51
dear, I don't care to renovate the house just for a three months'
rental."

"Then do let us go downstairs," I said. "There are such pretty 52
rooms there."

Then he took me in his arms and called me a blessed little goose, 53
and said he would go down cellar, if I wished, and have it white-
washed into the bargain.

But he is right enough about the beds and windows and things. 54

It is as airy and comfortable a room as anyone need wish, and, of 55
course, I would not be so silly as to make him uncomfortable just for
a whim.

I'm really getting quite fond of the big room, all but that horrid 56
paper.

Out of one window I can see the garden—those mysterious 57
deep-shaded arbors, the riotous old-fashioned flowers, and bushes
and gnarly trees.

Out of another I get a lovely view of the bay and a little private 58
wharf belonging to the estate. There is a beautiful shaded lane that
runs down there from the house. I always fancy I see people walking
in these numerous paths and arbors, but John has cautioned me not
to give way to fancy in the least. He says that with my imaginative
power and habit of story-making, a nervous weakness like mine is
sure to lead to all manner of excited fancies, and that I ought to use
my will and good sense to check the tendency. So I try.

I think sometimes that if I were only well enough to write a little 59
it would relieve the press of ideas and rest me.

But I find I get pretty tired when I try. 60

It is so discouraging not to have any advice and companionship 61
about my work. When I get really well, John says we will ask Cousin
Henry and Julia down for a long visit; but he says he would as soon
put fireworks in my pillow-case as to let me have those stimulating
people about now.

I wish I could get well faster. 62

But I must not think about that. This paper looks to me as if it 63
knew what a vicious influence it had!

There is a recurrent spot where the pattern lolls like a broken 64
neck and two bulbous eyes stare at you upside down.

I get positively angry with the impertinence of it and the ever- 65
lastingness. Up and down and sideways they crawl, and those
absurd unblinking eyes are everywhere. There is one place where
two breadths didn't match, and the eyes go all up and down the line,
one a little higher than the other.

I never saw so much expression in an inanimate thing before, 66
and we all know how much expression they have! I used to lie awake
as a child and get more entertainment and terror out of blank walls
and plain furniture than most children could find in a toy-store.

I remember what a kindly wink the knobs of our big old bureau 67
used to have, and there was one chair that always seemed like a
strong friend.

I used to feel that if any of the other things looked too fierce I 68
could always hop into that chair and be safe.

The furniture in this room is no worse than inharmonious, how- 69
ever, for we had to bring it all from downstairs. I suppose when this
was used as a playroom they had to take the nursery things out, and
no wonder! I never saw such ravages as the children have made here.

The wallpaper, as I said before, is torn off in spots, and it sticketh 70
closer than a brother[2]—they must have had perseverance as well as
hatred.

Then the floor is scratched and gouged and splintered, the plas- 71
ter itself is dug out here and there, and this great heavy bed, which is
all we found in the room, looks as if it had been through the wars.

But I don't mind it a bit—only the paper. 72

There comes John's sister. Such a dear girl as she is, and so care- 73
ful of me! I must not let her find me writing.

She is a perfect and enthusiastic housekeeper, and hopes for no 74
better profession. I verily believe she thinks it is the writing which
made me sick!

But I can write when she is out, and see her a long way off from 75
these windows.

There is one that commands the road, a lovely shaded winding 76
road, and one that just looks off over the country. A lovely country,
too, full of great elms and velvet meadows.

---

[2] *sticketh closer than a brother:* Proverbs 18:24.

This wallpaper has a kind of sub-pattern in a different shade, a 77 particularly irritating one, for you can only see it in certain lights, and not clearly then.

But in the places where it isn't faded and where the sun is just 78 so—I can see a strange, provoking, formless sort of figure that seems to skulk about behind that silly and conspicuous front design.

There's sister on the stairs! 79

Well, the Fourth of July is over! The people are all gone, and 80 I am tired out. John thought it might do me good to see a little company, so we just had Mother and Nellie and the children down for a week.

Of course I didn't do a thing. Jennie sees to everything now. 81

But it tired me all the same. 82

John says if I don't pick up faster he shall send me to Weir 83 Mitchell[3] in the fall.

But I don't want to go there at all. I had a friend who was in his 84 hands once, and she says he is just like John and my brother, only more so!

Besides, it is such an undertaking to go so far. 85

I don't feel as if it was worthwhile to turn my hand over for any- 86 thing, and I'm getting dreadfully fretful and querulous.

I cry at nothing, and cry most of the time. 87

Of course I don't when John is here, or anybody else, but when I 88 am alone.

And I am alone a good deal just now. John is kept in town very 89 often by serious cases, and Jennie is good and lets me alone when I want her to.

So I walk a little in the garden or down that lovely lane, sit on the 90 porch under the roses, and lie down up here a good deal.

I'm getting really fond of the room in spite of the wallpaper. 91 Perhaps *because* of the wallpaper.

It dwells in my mind so! 92

I lie here on this great immovable bed—it is nailed down, I 93 believe—and follow that pattern about by the hour. It is as good as gymnastics, I assure you. I start, we'll say, at the bottom, down in the corner over there where it has not been touched, and I determine for the thousandth time that I *will* follow that pointless pattern to some sort of a conclusion.

I know a little of the principle of design, and I know this thing 94 was not arranged on any laws of radiation, or alternation, or repetition, or symmetry, or anything else that I ever heard of.

---

[3] *Weir Mitchell:* See note on page 82.

It is repeated, of course, by the breadths, but not otherwise.   95

Looked at in one way, each breadth stands alone; the bloated   96
curves and flourishes—a kind of "debased Romanesque" with delir-
ium tremens go waddling up and down in isolated columns of fatuity.

But, on the other hand, they connect diagonally, and the sprawl-   97
ing outlines run off in great slanting waves of optic horror, like a lot
of wallowing sea-weeds in full chase.

The whole thing goes horizontally, too, at least it seems so, and I   98
exhaust myself trying to distinguish the order of its going in that
direction.

They have used a horizontal breadth for a frieze, and that adds   99
wonderfully to the confusion.

There is one end of the room where it is almost intact, and there,   100
when the crosslights fade and the low sun shines directly upon it, I
can almost fancy radiation after all—the interminable grotesque
seems to form around a common center and rush off in headlong
plunges of equal distraction.

It makes me tired to follow it. I will take a nap, I guess.   101

I don't know why I should write this.   102

I don't want to.   103

I don't feel able.   104

And I know John would think it absurd. But I *must* say what I   105
feel and think in some way—it is such a relief!

But the effort is getting to be greater than the relief.   106

Half the time now I am awfully lazy, and lie down ever so much.   107
John says I mustn't lose my strength, and has me take cod liver oil
and lots of tonics and things, to say nothing of ale and wine and rare
meat.

Dear John! He loves me very dearly, and hates to have me sick. I   108
tried to have a real earnest reasonable talk with him the other day,
and tell him how I wish he would let me go and make a visit to
Cousin Henry and Julia.

But he said I wasn't able to go, nor able to stand it after I got   109
there; and I did not make out a very good case for myself, for I was
crying before I had finished.

It is getting to be a great effort for me to think straight. Just this   110
nervous weakness, I suppose.

And dear John gathered me up in his arms, and just carried me   111
upstairs and laid me on the bed, and sat by me and read to me till it
tired my head.

He said I was his darling and his comfort and all he had, and that 112 I must take care of myself for his sake, and keep well.

He says no one but myself can help me out of it, that I must use 113 my will and self-control and not let any silly fancies run away with me.

There's one comfort—the baby is well and happy, and does not 114 have to occupy this nursery with the horrid wallpaper.

If we had not used it, that blessed child would have! What a for- 115 tunate escape! Why, I wouldn't have a child of mine, an impression-able little thing, live in such a room for worlds.

I never thought of it before, but it is lucky that John kept me here 116 after all; I can stand it so much easier than a baby, you see.

Of course I never mention it to them any more—I am too wise— 117 but I keep watch for it all the same.

There are things in that wallpaper that nobody knows about but 118 me, or ever will.

Behind that outside pattern the dim shapes get clearer every day. 119

It is always the same shape, only very numerous. 120

And it is like a woman stooping down and creeping about 121 behind that pattern. I don't like it a bit. I wonder—I begin to think— I wish John would take me away from here!

It is so hard to talk with John about my case, because he is so 122 wise, and because he loves me so.

But I tried it last night. 123

It was moonlight. The moon shines in all around just as the sun 124 does.

I hate to see it sometimes, it creeps so slowly, and always comes 125 in by one window or another.

John was asleep and I hated to waken him, so I kept still and 126 watched the moonlight on that undulating wallpaper till I felt creepy.

The faint figure behind seemed to shake the pattern, just as if she 127 wanted to get out.

I got up softly and went to feel and see if the paper *did* move, and 128 when I came back John was awake.

"What is it, little girl?" he said. "Don't go walking about like 129 that—you'll get cold."

I thought it was a good time to talk, so I told him that I really was 130 not gaining here, and that I wished he would take me away.

"Why, darling!" said he. "Our lease will be up in three weeks, 131 and I can't see how to leave before.

"The repairs are not done at home, and I cannot possibly leave 132 town just now. Of course, if you were in any danger, I could and would, but you really are better, dear, whether you can see it or not. I am a doctor, dear, and I know. You are gaining flesh and color, your appetite is better, I feel really much easier about you."

"I don't weigh a bit more," said I, "nor as much; and my appetite 133 may be better in the evening when you are here but it is worse in the morning when you are away!"

"Bless her little heart!" said he with a big hug. "She shall be as 134 sick as she pleases! But now let's improve the shining hours by going to sleep, and talk about it in the morning!"

"And you won't go away?" I asked gloomily. 135

"Why, how can I, dear? It is only three weeks more and then we 136 will take a nice little trip of a few days while Jennie is getting the house ready. Really, dear, you are better!"

"Better in body perhaps—" I began, and stopped short, for he sat 137 up straight and looked at me with such a stern, reproachful look that I could not say another word.

"My darling," said he, "I beg of you, for my sake and for our 138 child's sake, as well as for your own, that you will never for one instant let that idea enter your mind! There is nothing so dangerous, so fascinating, to a temperament like yours. It is a false and foolish fancy. Can you not trust me as a physician when I tell you so?"

So of course I said no more on that score, and we went to sleep 139 before long. He thought I was asleep first, but I wasn't, and lay there for hours trying to decide whether that front pattern and the back pattern really did move together or separately.

On a pattern like this, by daylight, there is a lack of sequence, a 140 defiance of law, that is a constant irritant to a normal mind.

The color is hideous enough, and unreliable enough, and infuri- 141 ating enough, but the pattern is torturing.

You think you have mastered it, but just as you get well under 142 way in following, it turns a back-somersault and there you are. It slaps you in the face, knocks you down, and tramples upon you. It is like a bad dream.

The outside pattern is a florid arabesque, reminding one of a fun- 143 gus. If you can imagine a toadstool in joints an interminable string of toadstools, budding and sprouting in endless convolutions—why, that is something like it.

That is, sometimes! 144

There is one marked peculiarity about this paper, a thing nobody 145 seems to notice but myself, and that is that it changes as the light changes.

When the sun shoots in through the east window—I always 146 watch for that first long, straight ray—it changes so quickly than I never can quite believe it.

That is why I watch it always. 147

By moonlight—the moon shines in all night when there is a 148 moon—I wouldn't know it was the same paper.

At night in any kind of light, in twilight, candlelight, lamplight, 149 and worst of all by moonlight, it becomes bars! The outside pattern, I mean, and the woman behind it is as plain as can be.

I didn't realize for a long time what the thing was that showed 150 behind, that dim sub-pattern, but now I am quite sure it is a woman.

By daylight she is subdued, quiet. I fancy it is the pattern that 151 keeps her so still. It is so puzzling. It keeps me quiet by the hour.

I lie down ever so much now. John says it is good for me, and to 152 sleep all I can.

Indeed he started the habit by making me lie down for an hour 153 after each meal.

It is a very bad habit, I am convinced, for you see, I don't sleep. 154

And that cultivates deceit, for I don't tell them I'm awake—oh, no! 155

The fact is I am getting a little afraid of John. 156

He seems very queer sometimes, and even Jennie has an inex- 157 plicable look.

It strikes me occasionally, just as a scientific hypothesis, that per- 158 haps it is the paper!

I have watched John when he did not know I was looking, and 159 come into the room suddenly on the most innocent excuses, and I've caught him several times *looking at the paper!* And Jennie too. I caught Jennie with her hand on it once.

She didn't know I was in the room, and when I asked her in a 160 quiet, a very quiet voice, with the most restrained manner possible, what she was doing with the paper, she turned around as if she had been caught stealing, and looked quite angry—asked me why I should frighten her so!

Then she said that the paper stained everything it touched, that 161 she had found yellow smooches on all my clothes and John's and she wished we would be more careful!

Did not that sound innocent? But I know she was studying that 162 pattern, and I am determined that nobody shall find it out but myself.

Life is very much more exciting now than it used to be. You see, 163 I have something more to expect, to look forward to, to watch. I really do eat better, and am more quiet than I was.

John is so pleased to see me improve! He laughed a little 164
the other day, and said I seemed to be flourishing in spite of my
wallpaper.

I turned it off with a laugh. I had no intention of telling him it 165
was *because* of the wallpaper—he would make fun of me. He might
even want to take me away.

I don't want to leave now until I have found it out. There is a 166
week more, and I think that will be enough.

I'm feeling so much better! 167

I don't sleep much at night, for it is so interesting to watch devel- 168
opments; but sleep a good deal during the daytime.

In the daytime it is tiresome and perplexing. 169

There are always new shoots on the fungus, and new shades of 170
yellow all over it. I cannot keep count of them, though I have tried
conscientiously.

It is the strangest yellow, that wallpaper! It makes me think of all 171
the yellow things I ever saw—not beautiful ones like buttercups, but
old, foul, bad yellow things.

But there is something else about that paper—the smell! I noticed 172
it the moment we came into the room, but with so much air and sun
it was not bad. Now we have had a week of fog and rain, and
whether the windows are open or not, the smell is here.

It creeps all over the house. 173

I find it hovering in the dining-room, skulking in the parlor, hid- 174
ing in the hall, lying in wait for me on the stairs.

It gets into my hair. 175

Even when I go to ride, if I turn my head suddenly and surprise 176
it—there is that smell!

Such a peculiar odor, too! I have spent hours in trying to analyze 177
it, to find what it smelled like.

It is not bad—at first—and very gentle, but quite the subtlest, 178
most enduring odor I ever met.

In this damp weather it is awful. I wake up in the night and find 179
it hanging over me.

It used to disturb me at first. I thought seriously of burning the 180
house—to reach the smell.

But now I am used to it. The only thing I can think of that it is like 181
is the *color* of the paper! A yellow smell.

There is a very funny mark on this wall, low down, near the 182
mopboard. A streak that runs round the room. It goes behind every
piece of furniture, except the bed, a long, straight, even *smooch*, as if
it had been rubbed over and over.

I wonder how it was done and who did it, and what they did it   183
for. Round and round and round—round and round and round—it
makes me dizzy!

I really have discovered something at last.   184

Through watching so much at night, when it changes so, I have   185
finally found out.

The front pattern *does* move—and no wonder! The woman   186
behind shakes it!

Sometimes I think there are a great many women behind, and   187
sometimes only one, and she crawls around fast, and her crawling
shakes it all over.

Then in the very bright spots she keeps still, and in the very   188
shady spots she just takes hold of the bars and shakes them hard.

And she is all the time trying to climb through. But nobody could   189
climb through that pattern—it strangles so; I think that is why it has
so many heads.

They get through and then the pattern strangles them off and   190
turns them upside down, and makes their eyes white!

If those heads were covered or taken off it would not be half so   191
bad.

I think that woman gets out in the daytime!   192

And I'll tell you why—privately—I've seen her!   193

I can see her out of every one of my windows!   194

It is the same woman, I know, for she is always creeping, and   195
most women do not creep by daylight.

I see her in that long shaded lane, creeping up and down. I see   196
her in those dark grape arbors, creeping all around the garden.

I see her on that long road under the trees, creeping along, and   197
when a carriage comes she hides under the blackberry vines.

I don't blame her a bit. It must be very humiliating to be caught   198
creeping by daylight!

I always lock the door when I creep by daylight. I can't do it at   199
night, for I know John would suspect something at once.

And John is so queer now that I don't want to irritate him. I wish   200
he would take another room! Besides, I don't want anybody to get
that woman out at night but myself.

I often wonder if I could see her out of all the windows at   201
once.

But, turn as fast as I can, I can only see out of one at a time.   202

And though I always see her, she *may* be able to creep faster than   203
I can turn! I have watched her sometimes away off in the open country, creeping as fast as a cloud shadow in a wind.

If only that top pattern could be gotten off from the under one! I 204
mean to try it, little by little.

I have found out another funny thing, but I shan't tell it this time! 205
It does not do to trust people too much.

There are only two more days to get this paper off, and I believe 206
John is beginning to notice. I don't like the look in his eyes.

And I heard him ask Jennie a lot of professional questions about 207
me. She had a very good report to give.

She said I slept a good deal in the daytime. 208

John knows I don't sleep very well at night, for all I'm so quiet! 209

He asked me all sorts of questions, too, and pretended to be very 210
loving and kind.

As if I couldn't see through him! 211

Still, I don't wonder he acts so, sleeping under this paper for 212
three months.

It only interests me, but I feel sure John and Jennie are affected 213
by it.

Hurrah! This is the last day, but it is enough. John is to stay in 214
town over night, and won't be out until this evening.

Jennie wanted to sleep with me—the sly thing; but I told her I 215
should undoubtedly rest better for a night all alone.

That was clever, for really I wasn't alone a bit! As soon as it was 216
moonlight and that poor thing began to crawl and shake the pattern,
I got up and ran to help her.

I pulled and she shook. I shook and she pulled, and before morn- 217
ing we had peeled off yards of that paper.

A strip about as high as my head and half around the room. 218

And then when the sun came and that awful pattern began to 219
laugh at me, I declared I would finish it today!

We go away tomorrow, and they are moving all my furniture 220
down again to leave things as they were before.

Jennie looked at the wall in amazement, but I told her merrily 221
that I did it out of pure spite at the vicious thing.

She laughed and said she wouldn't mind doing it herself, but I 222
must not get tired.

How she betrayed herself that time! 223

But I am here, and no person touches this paper but Me—not 223
alive!

She tried to get me out of the room—it was too patent! But I said 225
it was so quiet and empty and clean now that I believed I would

lie down again and sleep all I could, and not to wake me even for dinner—I would call when I woke.

So now she is gone, and the servants are gone, and the things are 226 gone, and there is nothing left but that great bedstead nailed down, with the canvas mattress we found on it.

We shall sleep downstairs tonight, and take the boat home 227 tomorrow.

I quite enjoy the room, now it is bare again. 228

How those children did tear about here! 229

This bedstead is fairly gnawed! 230

But I must get to work. 231

I have locked the door and thrown the key down into the front 232 path.

I don't want to go out, and I don't want to have anybody come 233 in, till John comes.

I want to astonish him. 234

I've got a rope up here that even Jennie did not find. If that 235 woman does get out, and tries to get away, I can tie her!

But I forgot I could not reach far without anything to stand on! 236

This bed will *not* move! 237

I tried to lift and push it until I was lame, and then I got so angry 238 I bit off a little piece at one corner—but it hurt my teeth.

Then I peeled off all the paper I could reach standing on the floor. 239 It sticks horribly and the pattern just enjoys it! All those strangled heads and bulbous eyes and waddling fungus growths just shriek with derision!

I am getting angry enough to do something desperate. To jump 240 out of the window would be admirable exercise, but the bars are too strong even to try.

Besides I wouldn't do it. Of course not. I know well enough that 241 a step like that is improper and might be misconstrued.

I don't like to *look* out of the windows even—there are so many 242 of those creeping women, and they creep so fast.

I wonder if they all came out of that wallpaper as I did? 243

But I am securely fastened now by my well-hidden rope—you 244 don't get *me* out in the road there!

I suppose I shall have to get back behind the pattern when it 245 comes night, and that is hard!

It is so pleasant to be out in this great room and creep around as 246 I please!

I don't want to go outside. I won't, even if Jennie asks me to. 247

For outside you have to creep on the ground, and everything is 248
green instead of yellow.

But here I can creep smoothly on the floor, and my shoulder just 249
fits in that long smooch around the wall, so I cannot lose my way.

Why, there's John at the door! 250

It is no use, young man, you can't open it! 251

How he does call and pound! 252

Now he's crying to Jennie for an axe. 253

It would be a shame to break down that beautiful door! 254

"John, dear!" said I in the gentlest voice. "The key is down by the 255
front steps, under a plantain leaf!"

That silenced him for a few moments. 256

Then he said, very quietly indeed, "Open the door, my darling!" 257

"I can't," said I. "The key is down by the front door under a plan- 258
tain leaf!" And then I said it again, several times, very gently and
slowly, and said it so often that he had to go and see, and he got it of
course, and came in. He stopped short by the door.

"What is the matter?" he cried. "For God's sake, what are you 259
doing!"

I kept on creeping just the same, but I looked at him over my 260
shoulder.

"I've got out at last," said I, "in spite of you and Jane. And I've 261
pulled off most of the paper, so you can't put me back!"

Now why should that man have fainted? But he did, and right 262
across my path by the wall, so that I had to creep over him every
time!

2

POETRY

BECAUSE I COULD NOT STOP FOR DEATH
Emily Dickinson

Because I could not stop for Death –
He kindly stopped for me –
The Carriage held but just Ourselves –
And Immortality.

We slowly drove – He knew no haste   5
And I had put away
My labor and my leisure too,
For His Civility –

We passed the School, where Children strove
At Recess – in the Ring –   10
We passed the Fields of Gazing Grain –
We passed the Setting Sun –

Or rather – He passed Us –
The Dews drew quivering and chill –
For only Gossamer,° my Gown –   15
My Tippet° – only Tulle° –

We passed before a House that seemed
A Swelling of the Ground –
The Roof was scarcely visible –
The Cornice – in the Ground –   20

---

15   thin fabric
16   cape, scarf; thin silk

Since then – tis Centuries – and yet
Feels shorter than the Day
I first surmised the Horses' Heads
Were toward Eternity –

MUCH MADNESS IS DIVINEST SENSE

Emily Dickinson

Much Madness is divinest Sense –
To a discerning Eye –
Much Sense – the starkest Madness –
'Tis the Majority
In this, as all, prevail –   5
Assent – and you are sane –
Demur – you're straightway dangerous –
And handled with a Chain –

MENDING WALL

Robert Frost

Something there is that doesn't love a wall,
That sends the frozen-ground-swell under it,
And spills the upper boulders in the sun;
And makes gaps even two can pass abreast.
The work of hunters is another thing: 5
I have come after them and made repair
Where they have left not one stone on a stone,
But they would have the rabbit out of hiding,
To please the yelping dogs. The gaps I mean,
No one has seen them made or heard them made, 10
But at spring mending-time we find them there.
I let my neighbor know beyond the hill;
And on a day we meet to walk the line
And set the wall between us once again.
We keep the wall between us as we go. 15
To each the boulders that have fallen to each.
And some are loaves and some so nearly balls
We have to use a spell to make them balance:
'Stay where you are until our backs are turned!'
We wear our fingers rough with handling them. 20
Oh, just another kind of outdoor game,
One on a side. It comes to little more:
There where it is we do not need the wall:
He is all pine and I am apple orchard.
My apple trees will never get across 25
And eat the cones under his pines, I tell him.
He only says, "Good fences make good neighbors."
Spring is the mischief in me, and I wonder
If I could put a notion in his head:
Why do they make good neighbors? Isn't it 30
Where there are cows? But here there are no cows."
Before I built a wall I'd ask to know
What I was walling in or walling out,
And to whom I was like to give offense.
Something there is that doesn't love a wall, 35
That wants it down. I could say "Elves" to him,

But it's not elves exactly, and I'd rather
He said it for himself. I see him there
Bringing a stone grasped firmly by the top
In each hand, like an old-stone savage armed.   40
He moves in darkness as it seems to me,
Not of woods only and the shade of trees.
He will not go behind his father's saying,
And he likes having thought of it so well
He says again, "Good fences make good neighbors."   45

DESIGN

Robert Frost

I found a dimpled spider, fat and white,
On a white heal-all,° holding up a moth
Like a white piece of rigid satin cloth—
Assorted characters of death and blight
Mixed ready to begin the morning right,   5
Like the ingredients of a witches' broth—
A snow-drop spider, a flower like a froth,
And dead wings carried like a paper kite.

What had that flower to do with being white,
The wayside blue and innocent heal-all?   10
What brought the kindred spider to that height,
Then steered the white moth thither in the night?
What but design of darkness to appall?—
If design govern in a thing so small.

---

2 *heal-all:* a flower, usually blue, thought to have healing powers.

THEME FOR ENGLISH B

Langston Hughes

The instructor said,
   Go home and write
   a page tonight.
   And let that page come out of you—
   Then, it will be true.   5

I wonder if it's that simple?

I am twenty-two, colored, born in Winston-Salem.
I went to school there, then Durham, then here
to this college on the hill above Harlem.°
I am the only colored student in my class.   10
The steps from the hill lead down to Harlem,
through a park, then I cross St. Nicholas,
Eighth Avenue, Seventh, and I come to the Y,
the Harlem Branch Y, where I take the elevator
up to my room, sit down, and write this page: 15

It's not easy to know what is true for you or me
at twenty-two, my age. But I guess I'm what
I feel and see and hear. Harlem, I hear you:
hear you, hear me—we two—you, me talk on this page.
(I hear New York, too.) Me—who?   20

Well, I like to eat, sleep, drink, and be in love.
I like to work, read, learn, and understand life.
I like a pipe for a Christmas present,
or records—Bessie,° bop,° or Bach.°

---

9   *college . . . Harlem:* a reference to Columbia University in the Columbia Heights section of New York City. The other streets and buildings mentioned in lines 11–14 refer to specific places in the same vicinity.

24   *Bessie:* Bessie Smith (ca. 1898–1937), American jazz singer, famed as the "Empress of the Blues." *bop:* a type of popular music that was in vogue in the 1940s through the 1960s. *Bach:* Johann Sebastian Bach (1685–1750), German composer, considered the master of the baroque style of music.

I guess being colored doesn't make me not like   25
the same things other folks like who are other races.
So will my page be colored that I write?
Being me, it will not be white.
But it will be
a part of you, instructor.   30
You are white—
yet a part of me, as I am a part of you.
That's American.

Sometimes perhaps you don't want to be a part of me.
Nor do I often want to be a part of you.   35
But we are, that's true!
As I learn from you,
I guess you learn from me—
although you're older—and white—
and somewhat more free.   40

This is my page for English B.

THOSE WINTER SUNDAYS

Robert Hayden

Sundays too my father got up early
and put his clothes on in the blueblack cold,
then with cracked hands that ached
from labor in the weekday weather made
banked fires blaze. No one ever thanked him.   5
I'd wake and hear the cold splintering, breaking,
When the rooms were warm, he'd call,
and slowly I would rise and dress,
fearing the chronic angers of that house,

Speaking indifferently to him,   10
who had driven out the cold
and polished my good shoes as well.
What did I know, what did I know
of love's austere and lonely offices?

THE EMPEROR OF ICE-CREAM

Wallace Stevens

Call the roller of big cigars,
The muscular one, and bid him whip
In kitchen cups concupiscent curds.
Let the wenches dawdle in such dress
As they are used to wear, and let the boys   5
Bring flowers in last month's newspapers.
Let be be finale° of seem.
The only emperor is the emperor of ice-cream.
Take from the dresser of deal,°
Lacking the three glass knobs, that sheet   10
On which she embroidered fantails° once

And spread it so as to cover her face.
If her horny feet protrude, they come
To show how cold she is, and dumb.
Let the lamp affix its beam.   15
The only emperor is the emperor of ice-cream.

---

7 *finale:* the grand conclusion.
9 *deal:* unfinished pine or fir used to make cheap furniture.
11 *fantails:* fantail pigeons.

MUSÉE DES BEAUX ARTS°

W. H. Auden

About suffering they were never wrong,
The Old Masters: how well they understood
Its human position; how it takes place
While someone else is eating or opening a window or just
    walking dully along;
How, when the aged are reverently, passionately waiting   5
For the miraculous birth, there always must be
Children who did not specially want it to happen, skating
On a pond at the edge of the wood:
They never forgot
That even the dreadful martyrdom must run its course   10
Anyhow in a corner, some untidy spot
Where the dogs go on with their doggy life and the
    torturer's horse
Scratches its innocent behind on a tree.
In Brueghel's *Icarus*, for instance: how everything turns
    away
Quite leisurely from the disaster; the ploughman may   15
Have heard the splash, the forsaken cry,
But for him it was not an important failure; the sun shone
As it had to on the white legs disappearing into the green
Water; and the expensive delicate ship that must have seen
Something amazing, a boy falling out of the sky,   20
Had somewhere to get to and sailed calmly on.

Musée des Beaux Arts   "Museum of Fine Arts."

WE REAL COOL

Gwendolyn Brooks

We real cool. We
Left school. We

Lurk late. We
Strike straight. We

Sing sin. We   5
Thin gin. We

Jazz June. We
Die soon.

THE RED WHEELBARROW
William Carlos Williams

so much depends
upon

a red wheel
barrow

glazed with rain   5
water

beside the white
chickens.

THE TYGER°

William Blake

Tyger! Tyger! burning bright
In the forests of the night,
What immortal hand or eye
Could frame thy fearful symmetry?

In what distant deeps or skies   5
Burnt the fire of thine eyes?
On what wings dare he aspire?
What the hand, dare seize the fire?

And what shoulder, & what art,
Could twist the sinews of thy heart?   10
And when thy heart began to beat,
What dread hand? & what dread feet?

What the hammer? what the chain?
In what furnace was thy brain?
What the anvil? what dread grasp   15
Dare its deadly terrors clasp?

When the stars threw down their spears,
And water'd heaven with their tears,
Did he smile his work to see?
Did he who made the Lamb make thee?   20

Tyger! Tyger! burning bright
In the forests of the night,
What immortal hand or eye
Dare frame thy fearful symmetry?

The Tyger   The title refers not only to a tiger but to any large, wild, ferocious cat.

SONNET 116: LET ME NOT TO THE MARRIAGE OF TRUE MINDS

William Shakespeare

Let me not to the marriage of true minds
Admit impediments.° Love is not love
Which alters when it alteration finds,
Or bends with the remover to remove:
Oh, no! it is an ever-fixéd mark,   5
That looks on tempests and is never shaken;
It is the star to every wandering bark,
Whose worth's unknown, although his height° be taken
Love's not Time's fool,° though rosy lips and cheeks
Within his° bending sickle's compass come;   10
Love alters not with his brief hours and weeks,
But bears it out even to the edge of doom.°
If this be error and upon me proved,
I never writ, nor no man ever loved.

---

2 *impediments:* a reference to "The Order of Solemnization of Matrimony" in the Anglican Church's *Book of Common Prayer:* "I require that if either of you know of any impediment why ye may not be lawfully joined together in Matrimony, ye do now confess it."
8 its altitude
9 slave
10 Time's
12 the Last Judgment

111

Sonnet 55: Not Marble, Nor the Gilded Monuments

William Shakespeare

Not marble, nor the gilded monuments
Of princes, shall outlive this powerful rhyme;
But you shall shine more bright in these contents
Than unswept stone, besmeared with sluttish time.
When wasteful war shall statues overturn,   5
And broils root out the work of masonry,
Nor° Mars his° sword nor war's quick fire shall burn
The living record of your memory.
'Gainst death and all-oblivious enmity
Shall you pace forth; your praise shall still find room   10
Even in the eyes of all posterity
That wear this world out to the ending doom.°
So, till the judgment that yourself arise,
You live in this, and dwell in lovers' eyes.

---

7   Neither; Mars's
12   Judgment Day

I HEAR AMERICA SINGING

Walt Whitman

I hear America singing, the varied carols I hear:
Those of mechanics—each one singing his, as it should be,
    blithe and strong;
The carpenter singing his, as he measures his plank or
    beam,
The mason singing his, as he makes ready for work, or
    leaves off work;
The boatman singing what belongs to him in his boat—the   5
    deckhand singing on the steamboat deck;
The shoemaker singing as he sits on his bench—the hatter
    singing as he stands;
The wood cutter's song—the ploughboy's on his way in
    the morning, or at noon intermissions, or at sun-
    down;
The delicious singing of the mother—or of the young wife
    at work—or of the girl sewing or washing—
Each singing what belongs to him or her and to none else;
The day what belongs to the day—at night, the part of   10
    young fellows, robust, friendly,
Singing, with open mouths, their strong melodious songs.

LEDA AND THE SWAN

William Butler Yeats

A sudden blow: the great wings beating still
Above the staggering girl, her thighs caressed
By the dark webs, her nape caught in his bill,
He holds her helpless breast upon his breast.

How can those terrified vague fingers push   5
The feathered glory from her loosening thighs?
And how can body, laid in that white rush,
But feel the strange heart beating where it lies?

A shudder in the loins engenders there
The broken wall, the burning roof and tower   10
And Agamemnon dead.
        Being so caught up,
So mastered by the brute blood of the air,
Did she put on his knowledge with his power
Before the indifferent beak could let her drop?   15

THE GOOD MORROW

John Donne

I wonder, by my troth, what thou and I
Did, till we loved! Were we not weaned till then,
But sucked on country pleasures, childishly?
Or snorted we in the seven sleepers' den?°
T'was so; But this, all pleasures fancies be.   5
If ever any beauty I did see,
Which I desired, and got, t'was but a dream of thee.

And now good morrow to our waking souls,
Which watch not one another out of fear;
For love all love of other sights controls,°   10
And makes one little room an everywhere.
Let sea-discoverers to new worlds have gone,
Let maps to other, worlds on worlds have shown,°
Let us possess one world; each hath one, and is one.

My face in thine eye, thine in mine appears,°   15
And true plain hearts do in the faces rest;
Where can we find two better hemispheres
Without sharp North, without declining West?
Whatever dies was not mixed equally;
If our two loves be one, or thou and I   20
Love so alike, that none do slacken, none can die.°

---

4 *seven sleepers' den:* a reference to the miraculous legend of the Seven Sleepers of Ephesus, in
Asia Minor. Seven young nobles fled Ephesus to avoid religious persecution by the Emperor
Decius (ca. 250 C.E.). They took refuge in a cave and were sealed inside. They then slept for
either 230 or 309 years, and they emerged praising God. After they died, their remains were
taken to St. Victor's Church in Marseilles, France, where they were encrypted.
10 *For love . . . controls:* i.e., Love is so powerful that it eliminates fear and makes everything in
the world worthy of love.
13, 14 *let sea-discoverers . . . shown:* i.e., let sea-explorers discover new worlds, and let maps
show other new worlds to other discovers.
15 *My face . . . appears:* Each face is reflected in the pupils of the other lover's eyes.
19–21 *Whatever . . . can die:* Scholastic philosophy argued that elements which are united in
perfect balance will never change or decay; hence, such a mixture cannot die. Donne's analogy
suggests—humorously—that the love of the lovers is too pure to die, and that they may therefore go on making love forever.

London, 1802

William Wordsworth

Milton! thou should'st be living at this hour:
England hath need of thee: she is a fen°
Of stagnant waters: altar, sword, and pen,
Fireside, the heroic wealth of hall and bower,
Have forfeited their ancient English dower°   5
Of inward happiness. We are selfish men;
Oh! raise us up, return to us again;
And give us manners,° virtue, freedom, power.
Thy soul was like a star, and dwelt apart:
Thou hadst a voice whose sound was like the sea: 10
Pure as the naked heavens, majestic, free,
So didst thou travel on life's common way,
In cheerful godliness; and yet thy heart
The lowliest duties on herself did lay.

---

2 bog, marsh
5 widow's inheritance
8 *manners:* customs, moral codes of social and political conduct.

ODE TO A NIGHTINGALE

John Keats

1

My heart aches, and a drowsy numbness pain
   My sense, as though of hemlock° I had drunk,
Or emptied some dull opiate to the drains
   One minute past, and Lethe-wards° had sunk:
'Tis not through envy of thy happy lot,   5
   But being too happy in thine happiness,—
      That thou, light-winged Dryad° of the trees,
         In some melodious plot
   Of beechen green, and shadows numberless,
Singest of summer in full-throated ease.   10

2

O, for a draught of vintage! that hath been
   Cool'd a long age in the deep-delved earth,
Tasting of Flora° and the country green,
   Dance, and Provencal song, and sunburnt mirth!
O for a beaker full of the warm South,   15
   Full of the true, the blushful Hippocrene,°
      With beaded bubbles winking at the brim,
         And purple-stainèd mouth;
   That I might drink, and leave the world unseen,
And with thee fade away into the forest dim: 20

---

2   a poisonous herb

4   *Lethe-wards:* toward the river of forgetfulness in Hades, the underworld of Greek mythology.

7   *Dryad:* in Greek mythology, a semidivine tree spirit.

13   *Flora:* the Roman goddess of flowers.

16   *Hippocrene:* the fountain of the Muses on Mt. Helicon in Greek mythology; the phrase thus refers to both the waters of poetic inspiration and a cup of wine.

3

Fade far away, dissolve, and quite forget
 What thou among the leaves hast never known,
The weariness, the fever, and the fret
 Here, where men sit and hear each other groan;
Where palsy shakes a few, sad, last gray hairs,   25
 Where youth grows pale, and spectre-thin, and dies;
  Where but to think is to be full of sorrow
   And leaden-eyed despairs,
  Where Beauty cannot keep her lustrous eyes,
Or new Love pine at them beyond to-morrow.   30

4

Away! away! for I will fly to thee,
 Not charioted by Bacchus° and his pards,°
But on the viewless wings of Poesy,°
 Though the dull brain perplexes and retards:
Already with thee! tender is the night,   35
 And haply the Queen-Moon is on her throne,
  Cluster'd around by all her starry Fays;°
   But here there is no light,
 Save what from heaven is with the breezes blown
Through verdurous glooms and winding mossy ways.   40

5

I cannot see what flowers are at my feet,
 Nor what soft incense hangs upon the boughs,
But, in embalmed° darkness, guess each sweet
 Wherewith the seasonable month endows
The grass, the thicket, and the fruit-tree wild;   45
 White hawthorn, and the pastoral eglantine;°
  Fast fading violets cover'd up in leaves;
   And mid-May's eldest child,

---

32 *Bacchus:* the Greek god of wine; leopards
33 poetry
37 fairies
43 fragrant
46 honeysuckle

The coming musk-rose, full of dewy wine,
The murmurous haunt of flies on summer eves.   50

6

Darkling° I listen; and, for many a time
I have been half in love with easeful Death,
Call'd him soft names in many a musèd rhyme,
To take into the air my quiet breath;
Now more than ever seems it rich to die,   55
To cease upon the midnight with no pain,
While thou art pouring forth thy soul abroad
In such an ecstasy!
Still wouldst thou sing, and I have ears in vain—
To thy high requiem become a sod.   60

7

Thou wast not born for death, immortal Bird!
No hungry generations tread thee down;
The voice I hear this passing night was heard
In ancient days by emperor and clown:
Perhaps the self-same song that found a path   65
Through the sad heart of Ruth,° when, sick for home,
She stood in tears amid the alien corn;°
The same that oft-times hath
Charm'd magic casements, opening on the foam
Of perilous seas, in faery lands forlorn.   70

8

Forlorn! the very word is like a bell
To toll me back from thee to my sole self!
Adieu! the fancy° cannot cheat so well
As she is fam'd to do, deceiving elf.

---

51   in the dark
66   *Ruth:* the widow of Boaz in the biblical Book of Ruth.
67   wheat, grain

Adieu! adieu! thy plaintive anthem fades
　Past the near meadows, over the still stream,
　　Up the hill-side; and now 'tis buried deep   75
　　　In the next valley-glades:
　Was it a vision, or a waking dream?
　Fled is that music:—Do I wake or sleep?

80

My Last Duchess°

Robert Browning

Ferrara

That's my last Duchess painted on the wall,
Looking as if she were alive. I call
That piece a wonder, now: Frà Pandolf's° hands   5
Worked busily a day, and there she stands.
Will't please you sit and look at her? I said
"Frà Pandolf" by design, for never read
Strangers like you that pictured countenance,
The depth and passion of its earnest glance,   10
But to myself they turned (since none puts by
The curtain I have drawn for you, but I)
And seemed as they would ask me, if they durst,°
How such a glance came there; so, not the first
Are you to turn and ask thus. Sir, 'twas not   15
Her husband's presence only, called that spot
Of joy into the Duchess' cheek: perhaps
Frà Pandolf chanced to say "Her mantle laps
Over my lady's wrist too much," or "Paint
Must never hope to reproduce the faint   20
Half-flush that dies along her throat": such stuff
Was courtesy, she thought, and cause enough
For calling up that spot of joy. She had
A heart—how shall I say?—too soon made glad,
Too easily impressed; she liked whate'er   25
She looked on, and her looks went everywhere.
Sir, 'twas all one! My favor at her breast,
The dropping of the daylight in the West,
The bough of cherries some officious fool
Broke in the orchard for her, the white mule   30
She rode with round the terrace—all and each
Would draw from her alike the approving speech,

MY LAST DUCHESS.   The poem is based on incidents in the life of Alfonso II, duke of Ferrara,
whose first wife died in 1561. Some claimed she was poisoned. The duke negotiated his second
marriage to the daughter of the count of Tyrol through an agent.
3   *Frà Pandolf:* an imaginary painter who is also a monk.
11   dared

Or blush, at least. She thanked men—good! but thanked
Somehow—I know not how—as if she ranked
My gift of a nine-hundred-years-old name
With anybody's gift. Who'd stoop to blame
This sort of trifling? Even had you skill   ·   35
In speech—(which I have not)—to make your will
Quite clear to such a one, and say, "Just this
Or that in you disgusts me; here you miss,
Or there exceed the mark"—and if she let
Herself be lessoned so, nor plainly set   40
Her wits to yours, forsooth, and made excuse
E'en then would be some stooping; and I choose
Never to stoop. Oh sir, she smiled, no doubt,
Whene'er I passed her; but who passed without
Much the same smile? This grew; I gave commands;   45
Then all smiles stopped together. There she stands
As if alive. Will't please you rise? We'll meet
The company below, then. I repeat,
The Count your master's known munificence
Is ample warrant that no just pretense   50
Of mine for dowry will be disallowed;
Though his fair daughter's self, as I avowed
At starting, is my object. Nay, we'll go
Together down, sir. Notice Neptune,° though,
Taming a sea horse, thought a rarity,   55
Which Claus of Innsbruck° cast in bronze for me!

---

54 *Neptune:* Roman god of the sea.
56 *Claus of Innsbruck:* an imaginary sculptor.

SONNETS FROM THE PORTUGUESE: NUMBER 14

Elizabeth Barrett Browning

If thou must love me, let it be for nought
Except for love's sake only. Do not say
"I love her for her smile—her look—her way
Of speaking gently—for a trick of thought
That falls in well with mine, and certes° brought   5
A sense of pleasant ease on such a day"—
For these things in themselves, Belovèd, may
Be changed, or change for thee,— and love, so wrought,°
May be unwrought so. Neither love me for
Thine own dear pity's wiping my cheeks dry,—   6
A creature might forget to weep, who bore
Thy comfort long, and lose thy love thereby!
But love me for love's sake, that evermore
Thou mayst love on, through love's eternity.

---

5 certainly
8 created

3

DRAMA

A DOLLHOUSE (ET DUKKEHJEM)

Henrik Ibsen
Translated by R. Farquharson Sharp

Characters

    Torvald Helmer, *a lawyer and bank manager*
    Nora, his wife
    Doctor Rank
    Mrs. Christine Linde
    Nils Krogstad, a lawyer and bank clerk
    Ivar, Bob, and *Emmy, the Helmers'* three young children
    Anne, their nurse
    Helen, a housemaid
    A Porter

The action takes place in HELMER'S apartment.

Act 1

SCENE. *A room furnished comfortably and tastefully, but not extravagantly. At the back, a door to the right leads to the entrance hall, another to the left leads to* HELMER'S *study. Between the doors stands a piano. In the middle of the left-hand wall is a door, and beyond it a window. Near the window are a round table, armchairs and a small sofa. In the right-hand wall, at the farther end, another door; and on the same side, nearer the footlights, a stove, two easy chairs and a rocking-chair; between the stove and the door, a small table. Engravings on the walls; a cabinet with china and other small objects; a small bookcase with well-bound books. The floors are carpeted, and a fire burns in the stove. It is winter.*

A bell rings in the hall; shortly afterwards the door is heard to open. Enter NORA, *humming a tune and in high spirits. She is in outdoor dress and carries a number of parcels; these she lays on the table to the right. She leaves the outer door open after her, and through it is seen a* PORTER *who is carrying a Christmas Tree and a basket, which he gives to the* MAID *who has opened the door.*

NORA.   Hide the Christmas Tree carefully, Helen. Be sure the children do not see it till this evening, when it is dressed. [*to the* PORTER, *taking out her purse..*] How much?

PORTER.   Sixpence.

NORA.   There is a shilling. No, keep the change. [*The* PORTER *thanks her, and goes out.* NORA *shuts the door. She is laughing to herself, as she takes off her hat and coat. She takes a packet of macaroons from her pocket and eats one or two; then goes cautiously to her husband's door and listens.*] Yes, he is in.

[*Still humming, she goes to the table on the right.*]

HELMER.   [*calls out from his room*] Is that my little lark twittering out there?

NORA.   [*busy opening some of the parcels*] Yes, it is!   5

HELMER.   Is my little squirrel bustling about?

NORA.   Yes!

HELMER.   When did my squirrel come home?

NORA.   Just now. [*puts the bag of macaroons into her pocket and wipes her mouth.*] Come in here, Torvald, and see what I have bought.

HELMER.   Don't disturb me. [*A little later, he opens the door and*   10
looks into the room, pen in hand.] Bought, did you say? All these things? Has my little spendthrift been wasting money again?

NORA.   Yes, but, Torvald, this year we really can let ourselves go a little. This is the first Christmas that we have not needed to economise.

HELMER.   Still, you know, we can't spend money recklessly.

NORA.   Yes, Torvald, we may be a wee bit more reckless now, mayn't we? Just a tiny wee bit! You are going to have a big salary and earn lots and lots of money.

HELMER.   Yes, after the New Year; but then it will be a whole quarter before the salary is due.

NORA.   Pooh! we can borrow till then.   15

HELMER.   Nora! [*goes up to her and takes her playfully by the ear.*] The same little featherhead! Suppose, now, that I borrowed fifty pounds to-day, and you spent it all in the Christmas week, and then on New Year's Eve a slate fell on my head and killed me, and—

NORA. [*putting her hands over his mouth*] Oh! don't say such horrid things.

HELMER. Still, suppose that happened—what then?

NORA. If that were to happen, I don't suppose I should care whether I owed money or not.

HELMER. Yes, but what about the people who had lent it?   20

NORA. They? Who would bother about them? I should not know who they were.

HELMER. That is like a woman! But seriously, Nora, you know what I think about that. No debt, no borrowing. There can be no freedom or beauty about a home life that depends on borrowing and debt. We two have kept bravely on the straight road so far, and we will go on the same way for the short time longer that there need be any struggle.

NORA. [*moving towards the stove*] As you please, Torvald.

HELMER. [*following her*] Come, come, my little skylark must not droop her wings. What is this! Is my little squirrel out of temper? [*taking out his purse.*]Nora, what do you think I have got here?

NORA. [*turning around quickly*] Money!   25

HELMER. There you are. [*gives her some money*] Do you think I don't know what a lot is wanted for housekeeping at Christmastime?

NORA. [*counting*] Ten shillings—a pound—two pounds! Thank you, thank you, Torvald; that will keep me going for a long time.

HELMER. Indeed it must.

NORA. Yes, yes, it will. But come here and let me show you what I have bought. And all so cheap! Look, here is a new suit for Ivar, and a sword; and a horse and a trumpet for Bob; and a doll and dolly's bedstead for Emmy—they are very plain, but anyway she will soon break them in pieces. And here are dress-lengths and handkerchiefs for the maids; old Anne ought really to have something better.

HELMER. And what is in this parcel?   30

NORA. [*crying out*] No, no! you mustn't see that till this evening.

HELMER. Very well. But now tell me, you extravagant little person, what would you like for yourself?

NORA. For myself? Oh, I am sure I don't want anything.

HELMER. Yes, but you must. Tell me something reasonable that you would particularly like to have.

NORA. No, I really can't think of anything—unless, Torvald—   35

HELMER. Well?

NORA. [*playing with his coat buttons, and without raising her eyes to his*] If you really want to give me something, you might—you might—

HELMER.   Well, out with it!

NORA.   [*speaking quickly*] You might give me money, Torvald. Only just as much as you can afford; and then one of these days I will buy something with it.

HELMER.   But, Nora—   40

NORA.   Oh, do! dear Torvald; please, please do! Then I will wrap it up in beautiful gilt paper and hang it on the Christmas Tree. Wouldn't that be fun?

HELMER.   What are little people called that are always wasting money?

NORA.   Spendthrifts—I know. Let us do as you suggest, Torvald, and then I shall have time to think what I am most in want of. That is a very sensible plan, isn't it?

HELMER.   [*smiling*] Indeed it is—that is to say, if you were really to save out of the money I give you, and then really buy something for yourself. But if you spend it all on the housekeeping and any number of unnecessary things, then I merely have to pay up again.

NORA.   Oh but, Torvald—   45

HELMER.   You can't deny it, my dear little Nora. [*puts his arm round her waist*] It's a sweet little spendthrift, but she uses up a deal of money. One would hardly believe how expensive such little persons are!

NORA.   It's a shame to say that. I do really save all I can.

HELMER.   [*laughing*] That's very true—all you can. But you can't save anything!

NORA.   [*smiling quietly and happily*] You haven't any idea how many expenses we skylarks and squirrels have, Torvald.

HELMER.   You are an odd little soul. Very like your father. You always find some new way of wheedling money out of me, and, as soon as you have got it, it seems to melt in your hands. You never know where it has gone. Still, one must take you as you are. It is in the blood; for indeed it is true that you can inherit these things, Nora.   50

NORA.   Ah, I wish I had inherited many of papa's qualities.

HELMER.   And I would not wish you to be anything but just what you are, my sweet little skylark. But, do you know, it strikes me that you are looking rather—what shall I say—rather uneasy to-day?

NORA.   Do I?

HELMER.   You do, really. Look straight at me.

NORA.   [*looks at him*] Well?   55

HELMER.   [*wagging his finger at her*] Hasn't Miss Sweet-Tooth been breaking rules in town to-day?

NORA.   No; what makes you think that?

HELMER. Hasn't she paid a visit to the confectioner's?

NORA. No, I assure you, Torvald— 60

HELMER. Not been nibbling sweets?

NORA. No, certainly not.

HELMER. Not even taken a bite at a macaroon or two?

NORA. No, Torvald, I assure you really—

HELMER. There, there, of course I was only joking. 65

NORA. [*going to the table on the right*] I should not think of going against your wishes.

HELMER. No, I am sure of that! besides, you gave me your word—[*going up to her*] Keep your little Christmas secrets to yourself, my darling. They will all be revealed to-night when the Christmas Tree is lit, no doubt.

NORA. Did you remember to invite Doctor Rank?

HELMER. No. But there is no need; as a matter of course he will come to dinner with us. However, I will ask him when he comes in this morning. I have ordered some good wine. Nora, you can't think how I am looking forward to this evening.

NORA. So am I! And how the children will enjoy themselves, 70
Torvald!

HELMER. It is splendid to feel that one has a perfectly safe appointment, and a big enough income. It's delightful to think of, isn't it?

NORA. It's wonderful!

HELMER. Do you remember last Christmas? For a full three weeks beforehand you shut yourself up every evening till long after midnight, making ornaments for the Christmas Tree and all the other fine things that were to be a surprise to us. It was the dullest three weeks I ever spent!

NORA. I didn't find it dull.

HELMER. [*smiling*] But there was precious little result, Nora. 75

NORA. Oh, you shouldn't tease me about that again. How could I help the cat's going in and tearing everything to pieces?

HELMER. Of course you couldn't, poor little girl. You had the best of intentions to please us all, and that's the main thing. But it is a good thing that our hard times are over.

NORA. Yes, it is really wonderful.

HELMER. This time I needn't sit here and be dull all alone, and you needn't ruin your dear eyes and your pretty little hands—

NORA. [*clapping her hands*] No, Torvald, I needn't any longer, 80
need I! It's wonderfully lovely to hear you say so! [*taking his arm*]
Now I will tell you how I have been thinking we ought to arrange

things, Torvald. As soon as Christmas is over—[*A bell rings in the hall.*] There's the bell. [*She tidies the room a little.*] There's someone at the door. What a nuisance!

HELMER. If it is a caller, remember I am not at home.

MAID. [*in the doorway*] A lady to see you, ma'am—a stranger.

NORA. Ask her to come in.

MAID. [*to HELMER*] The doctor came at the same time, sir.

HELMER. Did he go straight into my room? 85

MAID. Yes sir.

[*HELMER goes into his room. The MAID ushers in MRS. LINDE, who is in travelling dress, and shuts the door.*]

MRS. LINDE. [*in a dejected and timid voice*] How do you do, Nora?

NORA. [*doubtfully*] How do you do—

MRS. LINDE. You don't recognise me, I suppose.

NORA. No, I don't know—yes, to be sure, I seem to—[*suddenly*] 90 Yes! Christine! Is it really you?

MRS. LINDE. Yes, it is I.

NORA. Christine! To think of my not recognising you! And yet how could I—[*in a gentle voice*] How you have altered, Christine

MRS. LINDE. Yes, I have indeed. In nine, ten long years—

NORA. Is it so long since we met? I suppose it is. The last eight years have been a happy time for me, I can tell you. And so now you have come into the town, and have taken this long journey in winter—that was plucky of you.

MRS. LINDE. I arrived by steamer this morning. 95

NORA. To have some fun at Christmas-time, of course. How delightful! We will have such fun together! But take off your things. You are not cold, I hope. [*helps her*] Now we will sit down by the stove, and be cosy. No, take this arm-chair; I will sit here in the rocking-chair. [*takes her hands*] Now you look like your old self again; it was only the first moment—You are a little paler, Christine, and perhaps a little thinner.

MRS. LINDE. And much, much older, Nora.

NORA. Perhaps a little older; very, very little; certainly not much. [*stops suddenly and speaks seriously*] What a thoughtless creature I am, chattering away like this. My poor, dear Christine, do forgive me.

MRS. LINDE. What do you mean, Nora?

NORA. [*gently*] Poor Christine, you are a widow. 100

MRS. LINDE. Yes; it is three years ago now.

NORA. Yes, I knew; I saw it in the papers. I assure you, Christine, I meant ever so often to write to you at the time, but I always put it off and something always prevented me.

MRS. LINDE. I quite understand, dear.

NORA. It was very bad of me, Christine. Poor thing, how you must have suffered. And he left you nothing?

MRS. LINDE. No. 105

NORA. And no children?

MRS. LINDE. No.

NORA. Nothing at all, then?

MRS. LINDE. Not even any sorrow or grief to live upon.

NORA. [*looking incredulously at her*] But, Christine, is that 110 possible?

MRS. LINDE. [*smiles sadly and strokes her hair*] It sometimes happens, Nora.

NORA. So you are quite alone. How dreadfully sad that must be. I have three lovely children. You can't see them just now, for they are out with their nurse. But now you must tell me all about it.

MRS. LINDE. No, no; I want to hear you.

NORA. No, you must begin. I mustn't be selfish to-day; to-day I must only think of your affairs. But there is one thing I must tell you. Do you know we have just had a great piece of good luck?

MRS. LINDE. No, what is it? 115

NORA. Just fancy, my husband has been made manager of the Bank!

MRS. LINDE. Your husband? What good luck!

NORA. Yes, tremendous! A barrister's profession is such an uncertain thing, especially if he won't undertake unsavoury cases; and naturally Torvald has never been willing to do that, and I quite agree with him. You may imagine how pleased we are! He is to take up his work in the Bank at the New Year, and then he will have a big salary and lots of commissions. For the future we can live quite differently—we can do just as we like. I feel so relieved and so happy, Christine! It will be splendid to have heaps of money and not need to have any anxiety, won't it?

MRS. LINDE. Yes, anyhow I think it would be delightful to have what one needs.

NORA. No, not only what one needs, but heaps and heaps of 120 money.

MRS. LINDE. [*smiling*] Nora, Nora haven't you learnt sense yet? In our schooldays you were a great spendthrift.

NORA. [*laughing*] Yes, that is what Torvald says now. [*wags her finger at her*] But "Nora, Nora" is not so silly as you think. We have not been in a position for me to waste money. We have both had to work.

MRS. LINDE.   You too?

NORA.   Yes; odds and ends, needlework, crochet-work, embroidery, and that kind of thing. [*dropping her voice*] And other things as well. You know Torvald left his office when we were married? There was no prospect of promotion there, and he had to try and earn more than before. But during the first year he overworked himself dreadfully. You see, he had to make money every way he could, and he worked early and late; but he couldn't stand it, and fell dreadfully ill, and the doctors said it was necessary for him to go south.

MRS. LINDE.   You spent a whole year in Italy didn't you?   125

NORA.   Yes. It was no easy matter to get away, I can tell you. It was just as Ivar was born; but naturally we had to go. It was a wonderfully beautiful journey, and it saved Torvald's life. But it cost a tremendous lot of money, Christine.

MRS. LINDE.   So I should think.

NORA.   It cost about two hundred and fifty pounds. That's a lot, isn't it?

MRS. LINDE.   Yes, and in emergencies like that it is lucky to have the money.

NORA.   I ought to tell you that we had it from papa.   130

MRS. LINDE.   Oh, I see. It was just about that time that he died, wasn't it?

NORA.   Yes; and, just think of it, I couldn't go and nurse him. I was expecting little Ivar's birth every day and I had my poor sick Torvald to look after. My dear, kind father—I never saw him again, Christine. That was the saddest time I have known since our marriage.

MRS. LINDE.   I know how fond you were of him. And then you went off to Italy?

NORA.   Yes; you see we had money then, and the doctors insisted on our going, so we started a month later.

MRS. LINDE.   And your husband came back quite well?   135

NORA.   As sound as a bell!

MRS. LINDE.   But—the doctor?

NORA.   What doctor?

MRS. LINDE.   I thought your maid said the gentleman who arrived here just as I did was the doctor?

NORA.   Yes, that was Doctor Rank, but he doesn't come here   140 professionally. He is our greatest friend, and comes in at least once every day. No, Torvald has not had an hour's illness since then, and our children are strong and healthy and so am I. [*jumps up and claps her hands*] Christine! Christine! it's good to be alive and happy!—But how horrid of me; I am talking of nothing but my own affairs. [*sits on a stool near her, and rests her arms on her knees*] You mustn't be angry with me. Tell me, is it really true that you did not love your husband? Why did you marry him?

MRS. LINDE. My mother was alive then, and was bedridden and helpless, and I had to provide for my two younger brothers; so I did not think I was justified in refusing his offer.

NORA. No, perhaps you were quite right. He was rich at that time, then?

MRS. LINDE. I believe he was quite well off. But his business was a precarious one; and, when he died, it all went to pieces and there was nothing left.

NORA. And then?—

MRS. LINDE. Well, I had to turn my hand to anything I could 145 find—first a small shop, then a small school, and so on. The last three years have seemed like one long working-day, with no rest. Now it is at an end, Nora. My poor mother needs me no more, for she is gone; and the boys do not need me either; they have got situations and can shift for themselves.

NORA. What a relief you must feel it—

MRS. LINDE. No, indeed; I only feel my life unspeakably empty. No one to live for any more. [*gets up restlessly*] That was why I could not stand the life in my little backwater any longer. I hope it may be easier here to find something which will busy me and occupy my thoughts. If only I could have the good luck to get some regular work—office work of some kind—

NORA. But, Christine, that is so frightfully tiring, and you look tired out now. You had far better go away to some watering-place.

MRS. LINDE. [*walking to the window*] I have no father to give me money for a journey, Nora.

NORA. [*rising*] Oh, don't be angry with me. 150

MRS. LINDE. [*going up to her*] It is you that must not be angry with me, dear. The worst of a position like mine is that it makes one so bitter. No one to work for, and yet obliged to be always on the look-out for chances. One must live, and so one becomes selfish. When you told me of the happy turn your fortunes have taken—you will hardly believe it—I was delighted not so much on your account as on my own.

NORA. How do you mean?—Oh, I understand. You mean that perhaps Torvald could get you something to do.

MRS. LINDE.   Yes, that was what I was thinking of.

NORA.   He must, Christine. Just leave it to me; I will broach the subject very cleverly—I will think of something that will please him very much. It will make me so happy to be of some use to you.

MRS. LINDE.   How kind you are, Nora, to be so anxious to help   155
me! It is doubly kind in you, for you know so little of the burdens and troubles of life.

NORA.   I—? I know so little of them?

MRS. LINDE.   [*smiling*] My dear! Small household cares and that sort of thing!—You are a child, Nora.

NORA.   [*tosses her head and crosses the stage*] You ought not to be so superior.

MRS. LINDE.   No?

NORA.   You are just like the others. They all think that I am inca-   160
pable of anything really serious—

MRS. LINDE.   Come, come—

NORA.   —that I have gone through nothing in this world of cares.

MRS. LINDE.   But, my dear Nora, you have just told me all your troubles.

NORA.   Pooh!—those were trifles. [*lowering her voice*] I have not told you the important thing.

MRS. LINDE.   The important thing? What do you mean?   165

NORA.   You look down upon me altogether, Christine—but you ought not to. You are proud, aren't you, of having worked so hard and so long for your mother?

MRS. LINDE.   Indeed, I don't look down on any one. But it is true that I am both proud and glad to think that I was privileged to make the end of my mother's life almost free from care.

NORA.   And you are proud to think of what you have done for your brothers.

MRS. LINDE.   I think I have the right to be.

NORA.   I think so, too. But now, listen to this; I too have some-   170
thing to be proud of and glad of.

MRS. LINDE.   I have no doubt you have. But what do you refer to?

NORA.   Speak low. Suppose Torvald were to hear! He mustn't on any account—no one in the world must know, Christine, except you.

MRS. LINDE.   But what is it?

NORA.   Come here. [*pulls her down on the sofa beside her*] Now I will show you that I too have something to be proud and glad of. It was I who saved Torvald's life.

MRS. LINDE.   "Saved"? How?   175

NORA.   I told you about our trip to Italy. Torvald would never have recovered if he had not gone there—

MRS. LINDE.   Yes, but your father gave you the necessary funds.

NORA.   [*smiling*] Yes, that is what Torvald and all the others think, but—

MRS. LINDE.   But—

NORA.   Papa didn't give us a shilling. It was I who procured the   180 money.

MR. LINDE.   You? All that large sum?

NORA.   Two hundred and fifty pounds. What do you think of that?

MRS. LINDE.   But, Nora, how could you possibly do it? Did you win a prize in the Lottery?

NORA.   [*contemptuously*] In the Lottery? There would have been no credit in that.

MRS. LINDE.   But where did you get it from, then?   185

NORA.   [*humming and smiling with an air of mystery*] Hm, hm! Aha!

MRS. LINDE.   Because you couldn't have borrowed it.

NORA.   Couldn't I? Why not?

MRS. LINDE.   No, a wife cannot borrow without her husband's consent.

NORA.   [*tossing her head*] Oh, if it is a wife who has any head for   190 business—a wife who has the wit to be a little bit clever—

MRS. LINDE.   I don't understand it at all, Nora.

NORA.   There is no need you should. I never said I had borrowed the money. I may have got it some other way. [*lies back on the sofa*] Perhaps I got it from some other admirer. When anyone is as attractive as I am—

MRS. LINDE.   You are a mad creature.

NORA.   Now, you know you're full of curiosity, Christine.

MRS. LINDE.   Listen to me, Nora dear. Haven't you been a little   195 bit imprudent?

NORA.   [*sits up straight*] Is it imprudent to save your husband's life?

MRS. LINDE.   It seems to me imprudent, without his knowledge, to—

NORA.   But it was absolutely necessary that he should not know! My goodness, can't you understand that? It was necessary he should have no idea what a dangerous condition he was in. It was to me that the doctors came and said that his life was in danger, and that the only thing to save him was to live in the south. Do you suppose I didn't try, first of all, to get what I wanted as if it were for myself? I told him how much I should love to travel abroad like other young wives; I tried tears and entreaties with him; I told him that he ought to remember the condition I was in, and that he ought to be kind and indulgent to me; I even hinted that he might raise a loan. That nearly made him angry, Christine. He said I was thoughtless, and that it was his duty as my husband not to indulge me in my whims and caprices—as I believe he called them. Very well I thought, you must be saved—and that was how I came to devise a way out of the difficulty—

MRS. LINDE.   And did your husband never get to know from your father that the money had not come from him?

NORA.   No, never. Papa died just at that time. I had meant to let him into the secret and beg him never to reveal it. But he was so ill then—alas, there never was any need to tell him.   200

MRS. LINDE.   And since then have you never told your secret to your husband?

NORA.   Good Heavens, no! How could you think so? A man who has such strong opinions about these things! And besides, how painful and humiliating it would be for Torvald, with his manly independence, to know that he owed me anything! It would upset our mutual relations altogether; our beautiful happy home would no longer be what it is now.

MRS. LINDE.   Do you mean never to tell him about it?

NORA.   [*meditatively, and with a half smile*] Yes—some day, perhaps, after many years, when I am no longer as nice-looking as I am now. Don't laugh at me! I mean of course, when Torvald is no longer as devoted to me as he is now; when my dancing and dressing-up and reciting have palled on him; then it may be a good thing to have something in reserve—[*breaking off*] What nonsense! That time will never come. Now, what do you think of my great secret, Christine? Do you still think I am of no use? I can tell you, too, that this affair has caused me a lot of worry. It has been by no means easy for me to meet my engagements punctually. I may tell you that there is something that is called, in business, quarterly interest, and another thing called payment in instalments, and it is always so dreadfully difficult to manage them. I have had to save a little here and there, where I could, you understand. I have not been able to put aside much from my housekeeping money, for Torvald must have a good table. I couldn't let my children be shabbily dressed; I have felt obliged to use up all he gave me for them, the sweet little darlings!

MRS. LINDE. So it has all had to come out of your own neces- 205
saries of life, poor Nora?

NORA. Of course. Besides, I was the one responsible for it.
Whenever Torvald has given me the money for new dresses and such
things, I have never spent more than half of it; I have always bought
the simplest and cheapest things. Thank Heaven, any clothes look
well on me, and so Torvald has never noticed it. But it was often very
hard on me, Christine—because it is delightful to be really well
dressed, isn't it?

MRS. LINDE. Quite so.

NORA. Well, then I have found other ways of earning money.
Last winter I was lucky enough to get a lot of copying to do; so I
locked myself up and sat writing every evening until quite late at
night. Many a time I was desperately tired; but all the same it was a
tremendous pleasure to sit there working and earning money. It was
like being a man.

MRS. LINDE. How much have you been able to pay off in that
way?

NORA. I can't tell you exactly. You see, it is very difficult to keep 210
an account of a business matter of that kind. I only know that I have
paid every penny that I could scrape together. Many a time I was at
my wits' end. [*smiles*] Then I used to sit here and imagine that a rich
old gentleman had fallen in love with me—

MRS. LINDE. What! Who was it?

NORA. Be quiet!—that he had died; and that when his will was
opened it contained, written in big letters, the instruction: "The
lovely Mrs. Nora Helmer is to have all I possess paid over to her at
once in cash."

MRS. LINDE. But, my dear Nora—who could the man be?

NORA. Good gracious, can't you understand? There was no old
gentleman at all; it was only something that I used to sit here and
imagine, when I couldn't think of any way of procuring money. But
it's all the same now; the tiresome old person can stay where he is, as
far as I am concerned; I don't care about him or his will either, for I
am free from care now. [*jumps up*] My goodness, it's delightful to
think of, Christine! Free from care! To be able to be free from care,
quite free from care; to be able to play and romp with the children; to
be able to keep the house beautifully and have everything just as
Torvald likes it! And, think of it, soon the spring will come and the
big blue sky! Perhaps we shall be able to take a little trip—perhaps I
shall see the sea again! Oh, it's a wonderful thing to be alive and be
happy. [*A bell is heard in the hall*]

MRS. LINDE. [*rising*] There is the bell; perhaps I had better go.   215

NORA.   No, don't go; no one will come in here; it is sure to be for Torvald.

SERVANT.   [*at the hall door*] Excuse me, ma'am—there is a gentle-man to see the master, and as the doctor is with him—

NORA.   Who is it?

KROGSTAD.   [*at the door*] It is I, Mrs. Helmer. [*Mrs. Linde starts, trembles, and turns to the window.*]

NORA.   [*takes a step towards him, and speaks in a strained, low voice*]   220
You? What is it? What do you want to see my husband about?

KROGSTAD.   Bank business—in a way. I have a small post in the Bank, and I hear your husband is to be our chief now—

NORA.   Then it is—

KROGSTAD.   Nothing but dry business matters, Mrs. Helmer; absolutely nothing else.

NORA.   Be so good as to go into the study, then. [*She bows indif-ferently to him and shuts the door into the hall; then comes back and makes up the fire in the stove.*]

MRS. LINDE.   Nora—who was that man?   225

NORA.   A lawyer, of the name of Krogstad.

MRS. LINDE.   Then it really was he.

NORA.   Do you know the man?

MRS. LINDE.   I used to—many years ago. At one time he was a solicitor's clerk in our town.

NORA.   Yes, he was.   230

MRS. LINDE.   He is greatly altered.

NORA.   He made a very unhappy marriage.

MRS. LINDE.   He is a widower now, isn't he?

NORA.   With several children. There now, it is burning up.

[*Shuts the door of the stove and moves the rocking-chair aside.*]

MRS. LINDE.   They say he carries on various kinds of business.   235

NORA.   Really! Perhaps he does; I don't know anything about it. But don't let us think of business; it is so tiresome.

DOCTOR RANK.   [*comes out of HELMER'S study. Before he shuts the door he calls to him.*] No, my dear fellow, I won't disturb you; I would rather go in to your wife for a little while. [*shuts the door and sees MRS LINDE*] I beg your pardon; I am afraid I am disturbing you too.

NORA.   No, not at all. [*introducing him*] Doctor Rank, Mrs. Linde.

RANK.   I have often heard Mrs. Linde's name mentioned here. I think I passed you on the stairs when I arrived, Mrs. Linde?

MRS. LINDE.   Yes, I go up very slowly; I can't manage stairs well.   240
RANK.   Ah! some slight internal weakness?
MRS. LINDE.   No, the fact is I have been overworking myself.
RANK.   Nothing more than that? Then I suppose you have come
to town to amuse yourself with our entertainments?
MRS. LINDE.   I have come to look for work.
RANK.   Is that a good cure for overwork?   245
MRS. LINDE.   One must live, Doctor Rank.
RANK.   Yes, the general opinion seems to be that it is necessary.
NORA.   Look here, Doctor Rank—you know you want to live.
RANK.   Certainly. However wretched I may feel, I want to pro-
long the agony as long as possible. All my patients are like that. And
so are those who are morally diseased; one of them, and a bad case
too, is at this very moment with Helmer—
MRS. LINDE.   [*sadly*] Ah!   250
NORA.   Whom do you mean?
RANK.   A lawyer of the name of Krogstad, a fellow you don't
know at all. He suffers from a diseased moral character, Mrs. Helmer;
but even he began talking of its being highly important that he
should live.
NORA.   Did he? What did he want to speak to Torvald about?
RANK.   I have no idea; I only heard that it was something about
the Bank.
NORA.   I didn't know this—what's his name—Krogstad had   255
anything to do with the Bank.
RANK.   Yes, he has some sort of appointment there. [*to
MRS. LINDE*] I don't know whether you find also in your part of
the world that there are certain people who go zealously snuffing
about to smell out moral corruption, and, as soon as they have found
some, put the person concerned into some lucrative position where
they can keep their eye on him. Healthy natures are left out in the
cold.
MRS. LINDE.   Still I think the sick are those who most need taking care of.
RANK.   [*shrugging his shoulders*] Yes, there you are. That is the
sentiment that is turning Society into a sickhouse.

[*NORA, who has been absorbed in her thoughts, breaks out into smothered
laughter and claps her hands.*]

RANK.   Why do you laugh at that? Have you any notion what
Society really is?

NORA. What do I care about tiresome Society? I am laughing at 260
something quite different, something extremely amusing. Tell me,
Doctor Rank, are all the people who are employed in the Bank depen-
dent on Torvald now?

RANK. Is that what you find so extremely amusing?

NORA. [*smiling and humming*] That's my affair! [*walking about the
room*] It's perfectly glorious to think that we have—that Torvald has
so much power over so many people. [*takes the packet from her pocket*]
Doctor Rank, what do you say to a macaroon?

RANK. What, macaroons? I thought they were forbidden
here.

NORA. Yes, but these are some Christine gave me. 265

MRS. LINDE. What! I?—

NORA. Oh, well, don't be alarmed! You couldn't know that
Torvald had forbidden them. I must tell you that he is afraid they will
spoil my teeth. But, bah!—once in a way—That's so, isn't it, Doctor
Rank? By your leave? [*puts a macaroon into his mouth*] You must have
one too, Christine. And I shall have one, just a little one—or at most
two. [*walking about*] I am tremendously happy. There is just one thing
in the world now that I should dearly love to do.

RANK. Well, what is that?

NORA. It's something I should dearly love to say, if Torvald
could hear me.

RANK. Well, why can't you say it? 270

NORA. No, I daren't; it's so shocking.

MRS. LINDE. Shocking?

RANK. Well, I should not advise you to say it. Still, with us you
might. What is it you would so much like to say if Torvald could hear
you?

NORA. I should just love to say—Well, I'm damned!

RANK. Are you mad? 275

MRS. LINDE. Nora, dear—!

RANK. Say it, here he is!

NORA. [*hiding the packet*] Hush! Hush! Hush!

[*HELMER comes out of his room, with his coat over his arm and his hat in his
hands.*]

NORA. Well, Torvald dear, have you got rid of him?

HELMER. Yes, he has just gone. 280

NORA. Let me introduce you—this is Christine, who has come
to town.

HELMER. Christine—? Excuse me, but I don't know—

NORA.   Mrs. Linde, dear; Christine Linde.

HELMER.   Of course. A school friend of my wife's, I presume?

MRS. LINDE.   Yes, we have known each other since then.

NORA.   And just think, she has taken a long journey in order to   285
see you.

HELMER.   What do you mean?

MRS. LINDE.   No, really, I—

NORA.   Christine is tremendously clever at book-keeping, and
she is frightfully anxious to work under some clever man, so as to
perfect herself—

HELMER.   Very sensible, Mrs. Linde.

NORA.   And when she heard you had been appointed manager   290
of the Bank—the news was telegraphed, you know—she travelled
here as quick as she could. Torvald, I am sure you will be able to do
something for Christine, for my sake, won't you?

HELMER.   Well, it is not altogether impossible. I presume you are
a widow, Mrs. Linde?

MRS. LINDE.   Yes.

HELMER.   And have had some experience of book-keeping?

MRS. LINDE.   Yes, a fair amount.

HELMER.   Ah! well, it's very likely I may be able to find some-   295
thing for you—

NORA.   [*clapping her hands*] What did I tell you? What did I tell
you?

HELMER.   You have just come at a fortunate moment, Mrs.
Linde.

MRS. LINDE.   How am I to thank you?

HELMER.   There is no need. [*puts on his coat*] But to-day you must
excuse me—

RANK.   Wait a minute; I will come with you.   300

[*Brings his fur coat from the hall and warms it at the fire.*]

NORA.   Don't be long away, Torvald dear.

HELMER.   About an hour, not more.

NORA.   Are you going too, Christine?

MRS. LINDE.   [*putting on her cloak*] Yes, I must go and look for a
room.

HELMER.   Oh, well then, we can walk down the street together.   305

NORA.   [*helping her*] What a pity it is we are so short of space
here: I am afraid it is impossible for us—

MRS. LINDE.   Please don't think of it! Good-bye, Nora dear, and
many thanks.

NORA.   Good-bye for the present. Of course you will come back this evening. And you too, Dr. Rank. What do you say? If you are well enough? Oh, you must be! Wrap yourself up well.

[*They go to the door all talking together. Children's voices are heard on the staircase.*]

NORA.   There they are. There they are! [*She runs to open the door. The* NURSE *comes in with the children.*] Come in! Come in! [*stoops and kisses them*] Oh, you sweet blessings! Look at them, Christine! Aren't they darlings?

RANK.   Don't let us stand here in the draught.   310

HELMER.   Come along, Mrs. Linde; the place will only be bearable for a mother now!

[RANK, HELMER *and* MRS. LINDE *go downstairs. The* NURSE *comes forward with the children;* NORA *shuts the hall door.*]

NORA.   How fresh and well you look! Such red cheeks!—like apples and roses. [*The children all talk at once while she speaks to them.*] Have you had great fun? That's splendid! What, you pulled both Emmy and Bob along on the sledge?—both at once?—that *was* good. You are a clever boy, Ivar. Let me take her for a little, Anne. My sweet little baby doll! [*takes the baby from the* MAID *and dances it up and down*] Yes, yes, mother will dance with Bob too. What! Have you been snowballing? I wish I had been there too! No, no, I will take their things off, Anne; please let me do it, it is such fun. Go in now, you look half frozen. There is some coffee for you on the stove.

[*The* NURSE *goes into the room on the left.* NORA *takes off the children's things and throws them about, while they all talk to her at once.*]

NORA.   Really! Did a big dog run after you? But it didn't bite you? No, dogs don't bite nice little dolly children. You mustn't look at the parcels, Ivar. What are they? Ah, I daresay you would like to know. No, no—it's something nasty! Come, let us have a game! What shall we play at? Hide and Seek? Yes, we'll play Hide and Seek. Bob shall hide first. Must I hide? Very well, I'll hide first.

[*She and the children laugh and shout, and romp in and out of the room; at last* NORA *hides under the table, the children rush in and look for her, but do not see her; they hear her smothered laughter, run to the table, lift up the cloth and find her. Shouts of laughter. She crawls forward and pretends to frighten them. Fresh laughter. Meanwhile there has been a knock at the hall door, but none of them has noticed it. The door is half opened, and* KROGSTAD *appears. He waits a little; the game goes on.*]

KROGSTAD. Excuse me, Mrs. Helmer.

NORA. [*with a stifled cry, turns round and gets up on to her knees*] 315
Ah! what do you want?

KROGSTAD. Excuse me, the outer door was ajar; I suppose someone forgot to shut it.

NORA. [*rising*] My husband is out, Mr. Krogstad.

KROGSTAD. I know that.

NORA. What do you want here, then?

KROGSTAD. A word with you. 320

NORA. With me?—[*to the children, gently*] Go in to nurse. What? No, the strange man won't do mother any harm. When he has gone we will have another game. [*She takes the children into the room on the left, and shuts the door after them.*] You want to speak to me?

KROGSTAD. Yes, I do.

NORA. To-day? It is not the first of the month yet.

KROGSTAD. No, it is Christmas Eve, and it will depend on yourself what sort of a Christmas you will spend.

NORA. What do you want? To-day it is absolutely impossible 325
for me—

KROGSTAD. We won't talk about that till later on. This is something different. I presume you can give me a moment?

NORA. Yes—yes, I can—although—

KROGSTAD. Good. I was in Olsen's Restaurant and saw your husband going down the street—

NORA. Yes?

KROGSTAD With a lady. 330

NORA. What then?

KROGSTAD. May I make so bold as to ask if it was a Mrs. Linde?

NORA. It was.

KROGSTAD. Just arrived in town?

NORA. Yes, to-day. 335

KROGSTAD. She is a great friend of yours, isn't she?

NORA. She is. But I don't see—

KROGSTAD. I knew her too, once upon a time.

NORA. I am aware of that.

KROGSTAD. Are you? So you know all about it; I thought as 340
much. Then I can ask you, without beating about the bush—is Mrs. Linde to have an appointment in the Bank?

NORA.   What right have you to question me, Mr. Krogstad?— You, one of my husband's subordinates! But since you ask, you shall know. Yes, Mrs. Linde *is* to have an appointment. And it was I who pleaded her cause, Mr. Krogstad, let me tell you that.

KROGSTAD.   I was right in what I thought, then.

NORA.   [*walking up and down the stage*] Sometimes one has a tiny little bit of influence, I should hope. Because one is a woman, it does not necessarily follow that—. When anyone is in a subordinate position, Mr. Krogstad, they should really be careful to avoid offending anyone who—who—

KROGSTAD.   Who has influence?

NORA.   Exactly.   345

KROGSTAD.   [*changing his tone*] Mrs. Helmer, you will be so good as to use your influence on my behalf.

NORA.   What? What do you mean?

KROGSTAD.   You will be so kind as to see that I am allowed to keep my subordinate position in the Bank.

NORA.   What do you mean by that? Who proposes to take your post away from you?

KROGSTAD.   Oh, there is no necessity to keep up the pretence of   350 ignorance. I can quite understand that your friend is not very anxious to expose herself to the chance of rubbing shoulders with me; and I quite understand, too, whom I have to thank for being turned out.

NORA.   But I assure you—

KROGSTAD.   Very likely; but, to come to the point, the time has come when I should advise you to use your influence to prevent that.

NORA.   But, Mr. Krogstad, I *have* no influence.

KROGSTAD.   Haven't you? I thought you said yourself just now—

NORA.   Naturally I did not mean you to put that construction on   355 it. I! What should make you think I have any influence of that kind with my husband?

KROGSTAD.   Oh, I have known your husband from our student days. I don't suppose he is any more unassailable than other husbands.

NORA.   If you speak slightingly of my husband, I shall turn you out of the house.

KROGSTAD.   You are bold, Mrs. Helmer.

NORA.   I am not afraid of you any longer. As soon as the New Year comes, I shall in a very short time be free of the whole thing.

KROGSTAD.   [*controlling himself*] Listen to me, Mrs. Helmer. If   360 necessary, I am prepared to fight for my small post in the Bank as if I were fighting for my life.

Nora. So it seems.

Krogstad. It is not only for the sake of the money; indeed, that weighs least with me in the matter. There is another reason—well, I may as well tell you. My position is this. I daresay you know, like everybody else, that once, many years ago, I was guilty of an indiscretion.

Nora. I think I have heard something of the kind.

Krogstad. The matter never came into court; but every way seemed to be closed to me after that. So I took to the business that you know of. I had to do something; and, honestly, I don't think I've been one of the worst. But now I must cut myself free from all that. My sons are growing up; for their sake I must try and win back as much respect as I can in the town. This post in the Bank was like the first step up for me—and now your husband is going to kick me downstairs again into the mud.

Nora. But you must believe me, Mr. Krogstad; it is not in my power to help you at all. 365

Krogstad. Then it is because you haven't the will; but I have means to compel you.

Nora. You don't mean that you will tell my husband that I owe you money?

Krogstad. Hm!—suppose I were to tell him?

Nora. It would be perfectly infamous of you. [*sobbing*] To think of his learning my secret, which has been my joy and pride, in such an ugly, clumsy way—that he should learn it from you! And it would put me in a horribly disagreeable position—

Krogstad. Only disagreeable? 370

Nora. [*impetuously*] Well, do it, then!—and it will be the worse for you. My husband will see for himself what a blackguard you are, and you certainly won't keep your post then.

Krogstad. I asked you if it was only a disagreeable scene at home that you were afraid of?

Nora. If my husband does get to know of it, of course he will at once pay you what is still owing, and we shall have nothing more to do with you.

Krogstad. [*coming a step nearer*] Listen to me, Mrs. Helmer. Either you have a very bad memory or you know very little of business. I shall be obliged to remind you of a few details.

Nora. What do you mean? 375

Krogstad. When your husband was ill, you came to me to borrow two hundred and fifty pounds.

Nora. I didn't know any one else to go to.

Krogstad. I promised to get you that amount—

NORA. Yes, and you did so.

KROGSTAD. I promised to get you that amount, on certain 380
conditions. Your mind was so taken up with your husband's illness,
and you were so anxious to get the money for your journey, that you
seem to have paid no attention to the conditions of our bargain.
Therefore it will not be amiss if I remind you of them. Now, I
promised to get the money on the security of a bond which I drew
up.

NORA. Yes, and which I signed.

KROGSTAD. Good. But below your signature there were a few
lines constituting your father a surety for the money; those lines your
father should have signed.

NORA. Should? He did sign them.

KROGSTAD. I had left the date blank; that is to say your father
should himself have inserted the date on which he signed the paper.
Do you remember that?

NORA. Yes, I think I remember— 385

KROGSTAD. Then I gave you the bond to send by post to your
father. Is that not so?

NORA. Yes.

KROGSTAD. And you naturally did so at once, because five or six
days afterwards you brought me the bond with your father's signature. And then I gave you the money.

NORA. Well, haven't I been paying it off regularly?

KROGSTAD. Fairly so, yes. But—to come back to the matter 390
in hand—that must have been a very trying time for you, Mrs.
Helmer?

NORA. It was, indeed.

KROGSTAD. Your father was very ill, wasn't he?

NORA. He was very near his end.

KROGSTAD. And died soon afterwards?

NORA. Yes. 395

KROGSTAD. Tell me, Mrs. Helmer, can you by any chance
remember what day your father died?—on what day of the month, I
mean.

NORA. Papa died on the 29th of September.

KROGSTAD. That is correct; I have ascertained it for myself. And,
as that is so, there is a discrepancy [*taking a paper from his pocket*]
which I cannot account for.

NORA. What discrepancy? I don't know—

KROGSTAD. The discrepancy consists, Mrs. Helmer, in the fact 400
that your father signed this bond three days after his death.

NORA. What do you mean? I don't understand—

KROGSTAD. Your father died on the 29th of September. But, look here; your father has dated his signature the 2nd of October. It is a discrepancy, isn't it? [*NORA is silent.*] Can you explain it to me? [*NORA is still silent.*] It is a remarkable thing, too, that the words "2nd of October," as well as the year, are not written in your father's handwriting but in one that I think I know. Well, of course it can be explained; your father may have forgotten to date his signature, and someone else may have dated it haphazard before they knew of his death. There is no harm in that. It all depends on the signature of the name; and *that* is genuine, I suppose, Mrs. Helmer? It was your father himself who signed his name here?

NORA. [*after a short pause, throws her head up and looks defiantly at him*] No, it was not. It was I that wrote papa's name.

KROGSTAD. Are you aware that is a dangerous confession?

NORA. In what way? You shall have your money soon. 405

KROGSTAD. Let me ask you a question; why did you not send the paper to your father?

NORA. It was impossible; papa was so ill. If I had asked him for his signature, I should have had to tell him what the money was to be used for; and when he was so ill himself I couldn't tell him that my husband's life was in danger—it was impossible.

KROGSTAD. It would have been better for you if you had given up your trip abroad.

NORA. No, that was impossible. That trip was to save my husband's life; I couldn't give that up.

KROGSTAD. But did it never occur to you that you were 410 committing a fraud on me?

NORA. I couldn't take that into account; I didn't trouble myself about you at all. I couldn't bear you, because you put so many heartless difficulties in my way, although you knew what a dangerous condition my husband was in.

KROGSTAD. Mrs. Helmer, you evidently do not realise clearly what it is that you have been guilty of. But I can assure you that my one false step, which lost me all my reputation, was nothing more or nothing worse than what you have done.

NORA. You? Do you ask me to believe that you were brave enough to run a risk to save your wife's life?

KROGSTAD. The law cares nothing about motives.

NORA. Then it must be a very foolish law. 415

KROGSTAD. Foolish or not, it is the law by which you will be judged, if I produce this paper in court.

NORA.   I don't believe it. Is a daughter not to be allowed to spare her dying father anxiety and care? Is a wife not to be allowed to save her husband's life? I don't know much about law; but I am certain that there must be laws permitting such things as that. Have you no knowledge of such laws—you who are a lawyer? You must be a very poor lawyer, Mr. Krogstad.

KROGSTAD.   Maybe. But matters of business—such business as you and I have had together—do you think I don't understand that? Very well. Do as you please. But let me tell you this—if I lose my position a second time, you shall lose yours with me.

[*He bows, and goes out through the hall.*]

NORA.   [*appears buried in thought for a short time, then tosses her head*] Nonsense! Trying to frighten me like that!—I am not so silly as he thinks. [*begins to busy herself putting the children's things in order*] And yet—? No, it's impossible! I did it for love's sake.

THE CHILDREN.   [*in the doorway on the left*] Mother, the stranger 420 man has gone out through the gate.

NORA.   Yes, dears, I know. But, don't tell anyone about the stranger man. Do you hear? Not even papa.

CHILDREN.   No, mother; but will you come and play again?

NORA.   No, no—not now.

CHILDREN.   But, mother, you promised us.

NORA.   Yes, but I can't now. Run away in; I have such a lot to do. 425 Run away in, my sweet little darlings. [*She gets them into the room by degrees and shuts the door on them; then sits down on the sofa, takes up a piece of needlework and sews a few stitches, but soon stops.*] No! [*throws down the work, gets up, goes to the hall door and calls out*] Helen! bring the Tree in. [*goes to the table on the left, opens a drawer, and stops again*] No, no! it is quite impossible!

MAID.   [*coming in with the Tree*] Where shall I put it, ma'am?

NORA.   Here, in the middle of the floor.

MAID.   Shall I get you anything else?

NORA.   No, thank you. I have all I want.

[*Exit MAID.*]

NORA.   [*begins dressing the tree*] A candle here—and flowers 430 here—. The horrible man! It's all nonsense—there's nothing wrong. The Tree shall be splendid! I will do everything I can think of to please you, Torvald!—I will sing for you, dance for you—[*HELMER comes in with some papers under his arm*] Oh! are you back already?

HELMER.   Yes. Has anyone been here?

NORA.   Here? No.

HELMER.   That is strange. I saw Krogstad going out of the gate.

NORA.   Did you? Oh yes, I forgot, Krogstad was here for a moment.

HELMER.   Nora, I can see from your manner that he has been 435 here begging you to say a good word for him.

NORA.   Yes.

HELMER.   And you were to appear to do it of your own accord; you were to conceal from me the fact of his having been here; didn't he beg that of you too?

NORA.   Yes, Torvald, but—

HELMER.   Nora, Nora, and you would be a party to that sort of thing? To have any talk with a man like that, and give him any sort of promise? And to tell me a lie into the bargain?

NORA.   A lie—? 440

HELMER.   Didn't you tell me no one had been here? [*shakes his finger at her*] My little song-bird must never do that again. A song-bird must have a clean beak to chirp with—no false notes! [*puts his arm round her waist*] That is so, isn't it? Yes, I am sure it is. [*lets her go*] We will say no more about it. [*sits down by the stove*] How warm and snug it is here!

[*Turns over his papers.*]

NORA.   [*after a short pause, during which she busies herself with the Christmas Tree*] Torvald!

HELMER.   Yes.

NORA.   I am looking forward tremendously to the fancy dress ball at the Stenborgs' the day after to-morrow.

HELMER.   And I am tremendously curious to see what you are 445 going to surprise me with.

NORA.   It was very silly of me to want to do that.

HELMER.   What do you mean?

NORA.   I can't hit upon anything that will do; everything I think of seems so silly and insignificant.

HELMER.   Does my little Nora acknowledge that at last?

NORA.   [*standing behind his chair with her arms on the back of it*] Are 450 you very busy, Torvald?

HELMER.   Well—

NORA.   What are all those papers?

HELMER.   Bank business.

NORA.   Already?

HELMER.   I have got authority from the retiring manager to 455 undertake the necessary changes in the staff and in the rearrangement of the work; and I must make use of the Christmas week for that, so as to have everything in order for the new year.

NORA.   Then that was why this poor Krogstad—

HELMER.   Hm!

NORA.   [*leans against the back of his chair and strokes his hair*] If you hadn't been so busy I should have asked you a tremendously big favour, Torvald.

HELMER.   What is that? Tell me.

NORA.   There is no one has such good taste as you. And I do so 460 want to look nice at the fancy-dress ball. Torvald, couldn't you take me in hand and decide what I shall go as, and what sort of a dress I shall wear?

HELMER.   Aha! so my obstinate little woman is obliged to get someone to come to her rescue?

NORA.   Yes, Torvald, I can't get along a bit without your help.

HELMER.   Very well, I will think it over, we shall manage to hit upon something.

NORA.   That *is* nice of you. [*Goes to the Christmas Tree. A short pause.*] How pretty the red flowers look—. But, tell me, was it really something very bad that this Krogstad was guilty of?

HELMER.   He forged someone's name. Have you any idea what 465 that means?

NORA.   Isn't it possible that he was driven to do it by necessity?

HELMER.   Yes; or, as in so many cases, by imprudence. I am not so heartless as to condemn a man altogether because of a single false step of that kind.

NORA.   No you wouldn't, would you, Torvald?

HELMER.   Many a man has been able to retrieve his character, if he has openly confessed his fault and taken his punishment.

NORA.   Punishment—?   470

HELMER.   But Krogstad did nothing of that sort; he got himself out of it by a cunning trick, and that is why he has gone under altogether.

NORA.   But do you think it would—?

HELMER.   Just think how a guilty man like that has to lie and play the hypocrite with everyone, how he has to wear a mask in the presence of those near and dear to him, even before his own wife and children. And about the children—that is the most terrible part of it all, Nora.

NORA.   How?

HELMER.   Because such an atmosphere of lies infects and poi- 475
sons the whole life of a home. Each breath the children take in such a
house is full of the germs of evil.

NORA.   [*coming nearer him*] Are you sure of that?

HELMER.   My dear, I have often seen it in the course of my life as
a lawyer. Almost everyone who has gone to the bad early in life has
had a deceitful mother.

NORA.   Why do you only say—mother?

HELMER.   It seems most commonly to be the mother's influence,
though naturally a bad father's would have the same result. Every
lawyer is familiar with the fact. This Krogstad, now, has been persis-
tently poisoning his own children with lies and dissimulation; that is
why I say he has lost all moral character. [*holds out his hands to her*]
That is why my sweet little Nora must promise me not to plead his
cause. Give me your hand on it. Come, come, what is this? Give me
your hand. There now, that's settled. I assure you it would be quite
impossible for me to work with him; I literally feel physically ill
when I am in the company of such people.

NORA.   [*takes her hand out of his and goes to the opposite side* 480
of the Christmas Tree] How hot it is in here; and I have such a lot
to do.

HELMER.   [*getting up and putting his papers in order*] Yes, and I
must try and read through some of these before dinner; and I must
think about your costume, too. And it is just possible I may have
something ready in gold paper to hang up on the Tree. [*Puts his hand
on her head.*] My precious little singing-bird!

[*He goes into his room and shuts the door after him.*]

NORA.   [*after a pause, whispers*] No, no—it isn't true. It's impossible; it must be impossible.

[*The NURSE opens the door on the left.*]

NURSE.   The little ones are begging so hard to be allowed to
come in to mamma.

NORA.   No, no, no! Don't let them come in to me! You stay with
them, Anne. 485

NURSE.   Very well, ma'am.

[*Shuts the door.*]

NORA. [*pale with terror*] Deprave my little children? Poison my home? [*a short pause. Then she tosses her head.*] It's not true. It can't possibly be true.

Act 2

THE SAME SCENE. *The Christmas Tree is in the corner by the piano, stripped of its ornaments and with burnt-down candle-ends on its dishevelled branches. NORA's cloak and hat are lying on the sofa. She is alone in the room, walking about uneasily. She stops by the sofa and takes up her cloak.*

NORA. [*drops the cloak*] Someone is coming now! [*goes to the door and listens*] No—it is no one. Of course, no one will come to-day, Christmas Day—nor tomorrow either. But, perhaps—[*opens the door and looks out*] No, nothing in the letter-box; it is quite empty. [*comes forward*] What rubbish! of course he can't be in earnest about it. Such a thing couldn't happen; it is impossible—I have three little children.

[*Enter the NURSE from the room on the left, carrying a big cardboard box.*]

NURSE.   At last I have found the box with the fancy dress.

NORA.   Thanks; put it on the table.

NURSE.   [*doing so*] But it is very much in want of mending.

NORA.   I should like to tear it into a hundred thousand pieces.   5

NURSE.   What an idea! It can easily be put in order—just a little patience.

NORA.   Yes, I will go and get Mrs. Linde to come and help me with it.

NURSE.   What, out again? In this horrible weather? You will catch cold, ma'am, and make yourself ill.

NORA.   Well, worse than that might happen. How are the children?

NURSE.   The poor little souls are playing with their Christmas   10 presents, but—

NORA.   Do they ask much for me?

NURSE.   You see, they are so accustomed to have their mamma with them.

NORA.   Yes, but, nurse, I shall not be able to be so much with them now as I was before.

NURSE.   Oh well, young children easily get accustomed to anything.

NORA.   Do you think so? Do you think they would forget their   15 mother if she went away altogether?

NURSE. Good heavens!—went away altogether?

NORA. Nurse, I want you to tell me something I have often wondered about—how could you have the heart to put your own child out among strangers?

NURSE. I was obliged to, if I wanted to be little Nora's nurse.

NORA. Yes, but how could you be willing to do it?

NURSE. What, when I was going to get such a good place by it? 20 A poor girl who has got into trouble should be glad to. Besides, that wicked man didn't do a single thing for me.

NORA. But I suppose your daughter has quite forgotten you.

NURSE. No, indeed she hasn't. She wrote to me when she was confirmed, and when she was married.

NORA. [*putting her arms round her neck*] Dear old Anne, you were a good mother to me when I was little.

NURSE. Little Nora, poor dear, had no other mother but me.

NORA. And if my little ones had no other mother, I am sure you 25 would—What nonsense I am talking! [*opens the box*] Go in to them. Now I must—. You will see tomorrow how charming I shall look.

NURSE. I am sure there will be no one at the ball so charming as you, ma'am.

[*Goes into the room on the left.*]

NORA. [*begins to unpack the box, but soon pushes it away from her*] If only I dared go out. If only no one would come. If only I could be sure nothing would happen here in the meantime. Stuff and nonsense! No one will come. Only I mustn't think about it. I will brush my muff. What, lovely gloves! Out of my thoughts, out of my thoughts! One, two, three, four, five, six—[*Screams.*] Ah! there is someone coming—

[*Makes a movement towards the door, but stands irresolute.*]

[*Enter MRS, LINDE from the hall, where she has taken off her cloak and hat.*]

NORA. Oh, it's you, Christine. There is no one else out there, is there? How good of you to come!

MRS. LINDE. I heard you were up asking for me.

NORA. Yes, I was passing by. As a matter of fact, it is something 30 you could help me with. Let us sit down here on the sofa. Look here. To-morrow evening there is to be a fancy-dress ball at the Stenborgs', who live about us; and Torvald wants me to go as a Neapolitan fisher-girl, and dance the Tarantella that I learnt at Capri.

MRS. LINDE. I see; you are going to keep up the character.

NORA.   Yes, Torvald wants me to. Look, here is the dress; Torvald had it made for me there, but now it is all so torn, and I haven't any idea—

MRS. LINDE.   We will easily put that right. It is only some of the trimming come unsewn here and there. Needle and thread? Now then, that's all we want.

NORA.   It *is* nice of you.

MRS. LINDE.   [*sewing*] So you are going to be dressed up   35 to-morrow, Nora. I will tell you what—I shall come in for a moment and see you in your fine feathers. But I have completely forgotten to thank you for a delightful evening yesterday.

NORA.   [*gets up, and crosses the stages*] Well I don't think yesterday was a pleasant as usual. You ought to have come to town a little earlier, Christine. Certainly Torvald does understand how to make a house dainty and attractive.

MRS. LINDE.   And so do you, it seems to me; you are not your father's daughter for nothing. But tell me, is Doctor Rank always as depressed as he was yesterday?

NORA.   No; yesterday it was very noticeable. I must tell you that he suffers from a very dangerous disease. He has consumption of the spine, poor creature. His father was a horrible man who committed all sorts of excesses; and that is why his son was sickly from childhood, do you understand?

MRS. LINDE.   [*dropping her sewing*] But, my dearest Nora, how do you know anything about such things?

NORA.   [*walking about*] Pooh! When you have three children, you   40 get visits now and then from—from married women, who know something of medical matters, and they talk about one thing and another.

MRS. LINDE.   [*goes on sewing. A short silence*] Does Doctor Rank come here every day?

NORA.   Every day regularly. He is Torvald's most intimate friend, and a great friend of mine too. He is just like one of the family.

MRS. LINDE.   But tell me this—is he perfectly sincere? I mean, isn't he the kind of man that is very anxious to make himself agreeable?

NORA.   Not in the least. What makes you think that?

MRS. LINDE.   When you introduced him to me yesterday, he   45 declared he had often heard my name mentioned in this house; but afterwards I noticed that your husband hadn't the slightest idea who I was. So how could Doctor Rank—?

Nora. That is quite right, Christine. Torvald is so absurdly fond of me that he wants me absolutely to himself, as he says. At first he used to seem almost jealous if I mentioned any of the dear folk at home, so naturally I gave up doing so. But I often talk about such things with Doctor Rank, because he likes hearing about them.

Mrs. Linde. Listen to me, Nora. You are still very like a child in many things, and I am older than you in many ways and have a little more experience. Let me tell you this—you ought to make an end of it with Doctor Rank.

Nora. What ought I to make an end of?

Mrs. Linde. Of two things, I think. Yesterday you talked some nonsense about a rich admirer who was to leave you money—

Nora. An admirer who doesn't exist, unfortunately! But what then?   50

Mrs. Linde. Is Doctor Rank a man of means?

Nora. Yes, he is.

Mrs. Linde. And has no one to provide for?

Nora. No, no one; but—

Mrs. Linde. And comes here every day?   55

Nora. Yes, I told you so.

Mrs. Linde. But how can this well-bred man be so tactless?

Nora. I don't understand you at all.

Mrs. Linde. Don't prevaricate, Nora. Do you suppose I don't guess who lent you the two hundred and fifty pounds?

Nora. Are you out of your senses? How can you think of such   60 a thing! A friend of ours, who comes here every day! Do you realise what a horribly painful position that would be?

Mrs. Linde. Then it really isn't he?

Nora. No, certainly not. It would never have entered into my head for a moment. Besides, he had no money to lend then; he came into his money afterwards.

Mrs. Linde. Well, I think that was lucky for you, my dear Nora.

Nora. No, it would never have come into my head to ask Doctor Rank. Although I am quite sure that if I had asked him—

Mrs. Linde. But of course you won't.   65

Nora. Of course not. I have no reason to think it could possibly be necessary. But I am quite sure that if I told Doctor Rank—

Mrs. Linde. Behind your husband's back?

Nora. I must make an end of it with the other one, and that will be behind his back too. I *must* make an end of it with him.

Mrs. Linde. Yes, that is what I told you yesterday, but—

NORA.   [*walking up and down*] A man can put a thing like that 70 straight much easier than a woman—

MRS. LINDE.   One's husband, yes.

NORA.   Nonsense! [*standing still*] When you pay off a debt you get your bond back, don't you?

MRS. LINDE.   Yes, as a matter of course.

NORA.   And can tear it into a hundred thousand pieces, and burn it up—the nasty dirty paper!

MRS. LINDE.   [*looks hard at her, lays down her sewing and gets up* 75 *slowly*] Nora, you are concealing something from me.

NORA.   Do I look as if I were?

MRS. LINDE.   Something has happened to you since yesterday morning. Nora, what is it?

NORA.   [*going nearer to her*] Christine! [*listens*] Hush! there's Torvald come home. Do you mind going in to the children for the present? Torvald can't bear to see dressmaking going on. Let Anne help you.

MRS. LINDE.   [*gathering some of the things together*] Certainly—but I am not going away from here till we have had it out with one another.

[*She goes into the room on the left, as* HELMER *comes in from the hall.*]

NORA.   [*going up to* HELMER] I have wanted you so much, 80 Torvald dear.

HELMER.   Was that the dressmaker?

NORA.   No, it was Christine; she is helping me to put my dress in order. You will see I shall look quite smart.

HELMER.   Wasn't that a happy thought of mine, now?

NORA.   Splendid! But don't you think it is nice of me, too, to do as you wish?

HELMER.   Nice?—because you do as your husband wishes? 85 Well, well, you little rogue, I am sure you did not mean it in that way. But I am not going to disturb you; you will want to be trying on your dress, I expect.

NORA.   I suppose you are going to work.

HELMER.   Yes. [*shows her a bundle of papers*] Look at that. I have just been into the bank. [*Turns to go into his room.*]

NORA.   Torvald.

HELMER.   Yes.

NORA.   If your little squirrel were to ask you for something very, 90 very prettily—?

HELMER.   What then?

NORA.   Would you do it?

HELMER.   I should like to hear what it is, first.

NORA.   Your squirrel would run about and do all her tricks if you would be nice, and do what she wants.

HELMER.   Speak plainly.   95

NORA.   Your skylark would chirp about in every room, with her song rising and falling—

HELMER.   Well, my skylark does that anyhow.

NORA.   I would play the fairy and dance for you in the moonlight, Torvald.

HELMER.   Nora—you surely don't mean that request you made of me this morning?

NORA.   [*going near him*] Yes, Torvald, I beg you so earnestly—   100

HELMER.   Have you really the courage to open up that question again?

NORA.   Yes, dear, you *must* do as I ask; you *must* let Krogstad keep his post in the Bank.

HELMER.   My dear Nora, it is his post that I have arranged Mrs. Linde shall have.

NORA.   Yes, you have been awfully kind about that; but you could just as well dismiss some other clerk instead of Krogstad.

HELMER.   This is simply incredible obstinacy! Because you chose   105
to give him a thoughtless promise that you would speak for him, I am expected to—

NORA.   That isn't the reason, Torvald. It is for your own sake. This fellow writes in the most scurrilous newspapers; you have told me so yourself. He can do you an unspeakable amount of harm. I am frightened to death of him—

HELMER.   Ah, I understand; it is recollections of the past that scare you.

NORA.   What do you mean?

HELMER.   Naturally you are thinking of your father.

NORA.   Yes—yes, of course. Just recall to your mind what these   110
malicious creatures wrote in the papers about papa, and how horribly they slandered him. I believe they would have procured his dismissal if the Department had not sent you over to inquire into it, and if you had not been so kindly disposed and helpful to him.

HELMER.   My little Nora, there is an important difference between your father and me. Your father's reputation as a public official was not above suspicion. Mine is, and I hope it will continue to be so, as long as I hold my office.

NORA. You never can tell what mischief these men may contrive. We ought to be so well off, so snug and happy here in our peaceful home, and have no cares—you and I and the children, Torvald! That is why I beg you so earnestly—

HELMER. And it is just by interceding for him that you make it impossible for me to keep him. It is already known at the Bank that I mean to dismiss Krogstad. Is it to get about now that the new manager has changed his mind at his wife's bidding—

NORA. And what if it did?

HELMER. Of course!—if only this obstinate little person can get 115 her way! Do you suppose I am going to make myself ridiculous before my whole staff, to let people think that I am a man to be swayed by all sorts of outside influence? I should very soon feel the consequences of it, I can tell you! And besides, there is one thing that makes it quite impossible for me to have Krogstad in the Bank as long as I am manager.

NORA. Whatever is that?

HELMER. His moral failings I might perhaps have overlooked, if necessary—

NORA. Yes, you could—couldn't you?

HELMER. And I hear he is a good worker, too. But I knew him when we were boys. It was one of those rash friendships that so often prove an incubus in after life. I may as well tell you plainly, we were once on very intimate terms with one another. But this tactless fellow lays no restraint on himself when other people are present. On the contrary, he thinks it gives him the right to adopt a familiar tone with me, and every minute it is "I say, Helmer, old fellow!" and that sort of thing. I assure you it is extremely painful for me. He would make my position in the Bank intolerable.

NORA. Torvald, I don't believe you mean that. 120

HELMER. Don't you? Why not?

NORA. Because it is such a narrow-minded way of looking at things.

HELMER. What are you saying? Narrow-minded? Do you think I am narrow-minded?

NORA. No, just the opposite, dear—and it is exactly for that reason.

HELMER. It's the same thing. You say my point of view is nar- 125 row-minded, so I must be so too. Narrow-minded! Very well—I must put an end to this. [*Goes to the hall-door and calls.*] Helen!

NORA. What are you going to do?

HELMER.   [*looking among his papers*] Settle it. [*Enter MAID.*] Look here; take this letter and go downstairs with it at once. Find a messenger and tell him to deliver it, and be quick. The address is on it, and here is the money.

MAID.   Very well, sir.

[*Exits with the letter.*]

HELMER.   [*putting his papers together*] Now then, little Miss Obstinate.

NORA.   [*breathlessly*] Torvald—what was that letter?   130

HELMER.   Krogstad's dismissal.

NORA.   Call her back, Torvald! There is still time. Oh Torvald, call her back! Do it for my sake—for your own sake—for the children's sake! Do you hear me, Torvald? Call her back!! You don't know what that letter can bring upon us.

HELMER.   It's too late.

NORA.   Yes, it's too late.

HELMER.   My dear Nora, I can forgive the anxiety you are in,   135 although really it is an insult to me. It is, indeed. Isn't it an insult to think that I should be afraid of a starving quill-driver's vengeance? But I forgive you nevertheless, because it is such eloquent witness to your great love for me. [*takes her in his arms*] And that is as it should be, my own darling Nora. Come what will, you may be sure I shall have both courage and strength if they be needed. You will see I am man enough to take everything upon myself.

NORA.   [*in a horror-stricken voice*] What do you mean by that?

HELMER.   Everything, I say—

NORA.   [*recovering herself*] You will never have to do that.

HELMER.   That's right. Well, we will share it, Nora, as man and wife should. That is how it shall be. [*caressing her*] Are you content now? There! there!—not these frightened dove's eyes! The whole thing is only the wildest fancy!—Now, you must go and play through the Tarantella and practise with your tambourine. I shall go into the inner office and shut the door, and I shall hear nothing; you can make as much noise as you please. [*turns back at the door*] And when Rank comes, tell him where he will find me.

[*Nods to her, takes his papers and goes into his room, and shuts the door after him*]

NORA.   [*bewildered with anxiety, stands as if rooted to the spot, and*   140 *whispers*] He is capable of doing it. He will do it. He will do it in spite of everything.—No, not that! Never, never! Anything rather than that! Oh, for some help, some way out of it! [*The door-bell rings.*] Doctor Rank! Anything rather than that—anything, whatever it is!

[*She puts her hands over her face, pulls herself together, goes to the door and opens it.* RANK *is standing without, hanging up his coat. During the following dialogue it begins to grow dark.*]

NORA.   Good-day, Doctor Rank. I knew your ring. But you mustn't go in to Torvald now; I think he is busy with something.

RANK.   And you?

NORA.   [*brings him in and shuts the door after him*] Oh, you know very well I always have time for you.

RANK.   Thank you. I shall make use of as much of it as I can.

NORA.   What do you mean by that? As much of it as you can?   145

RANK.   Well, does that alarm you?

NORA.   It was such a strange way of putting it. Is anything likely to happen?

RANK.   Nothing but what I have long been prepared for. But I certainly didn't expect it to happen so soon.

NORA.   [*gripping him by the arm*] What have you found out? Doctor Rank, you must tell me.

RANK.   [*sitting down by the stove*] It is all up with me. And it can't   150 be helped.

NORA.   [*with a sigh of relief*] Is it about yourself?

RANK.   Who else? It is no use lying to one's self. I am the most wretched of all my patients, Mrs. Helmer. Lately I have been taking stock of my internal economy. Bankrupt! Probably within a month I shall lie rotting in the churchyard.

NORA.   What an ugly thing to say!

RANK.   The thing itself is cursedly ugly, and the worst of it is that I shall have to face so much more that is ugly before that. I shall only make one more examination of myself; when I have done that, I shall know pretty certainly when it will be that the horrors of dissolution will begin. There is something I want to tell you. Helmer's refined nature gives him an unconquerable disgust at everything that is ugly; I won't have him in my sick-room.

NORA.   Oh, but, Doctor Rank—   155

RANK.   I won't have him there. Not on any account. I bar my door to him. As soon as I am quite certain that the worst has come, I shall send you my card with a black cross on it, and then you will know that the loathsome end has begun.

NORA.   You are quite absurd to-day. And I wanted you so much to be in a really good humour.

RANK.   With death stalking beside me?—To have to pay this penalty for another man's sin! Is there any justice in that? And in every single family, in one way or another, some such inexorable retribution is being exacted—

NORA.   [*putting her hands over her ears*] Rubbish! Do talk of something cheerful.

RANK.   Oh, it's a mere laughing matter, the whole thing. My poor innocent spine has to suffer for my father's youthful amusements.

NORA.   [*sitting at the table on the left*] I suppose you mean that he was too partial to asparagus and pâté de foie gras, don't you.

RANK.   Yes, and to truffles.

NORA.   Truffles, yes. And oysters too, I suppose?

RANK.   Oysters, of course, that goes without saying.

NORA.   And heaps of port and champagne. It is sad that all these nice things should take their revenge on our bones.

RANK.   Especially that they should revenge themselves on the unlucky bones of those who have not had the satisfaction of enjoying them.

NORA.   Yes, that's the saddest part of it all.

RANK.   [*with a searching look at her*] Hm!—

NORA.   [*after a short pause*] Why did you smile?

RANK.   No, it was you that laughed.

NORA.   No, it was you that smiled, Doctor Rank!

RANK.   [*rising*] You are a greater rascal than I thought.

NORA.   I am in a silly mood to-day.

RANK.   So it seems.

NORA.   [*putting her hands on his shoulders*] Dear, dear Doctor Rank, death mustn't take you away from Torvald and me.

RANK.   It is a loss you would easily recover from. Those who are gone are soon forgotten.

NORA.   [*looking at him anxiously*] Do you believe that?

RANK.   People form new ties, and then—

NORA.   Who will form new ties?

RANK.   Both you and Helmer, when I am gone. You yourself are already on the high road to it, I think. What did that Mrs. Linde want here last night?

NORA.   Oho!—you don't mean to say you are jealous of poor Christine?

RANK.   Yes, I am. She will be my successor in this house. When I am done for, this woman will—

NORA. Hush! don't speak so loud. She is in that room.

RANK. To-day again. There, you see.

NORA. She has only come to sew my dress for me. Bless my 185
soul, how unreasonable you are! [*sits down on the sofa*] Be nice now,
Doctor Rank, and tomorrow you will see how beautifully I shall
dance, and you can imagine I am doing it all for you—and for
Torvald too, of course. [*takes various things out of the box*] Doctor Rank,
come and sit down here, and I will show you something.

RANK. [*sitting down*] What is it?

NORA. Just look at those!

RANK. Silk stockings.

NORA. Flesh-coloured. Aren't they lovely? It is so dark here
now, but to-morrow—. No, no, no! you must only look at the feet. Oh
well, you may have leave to look at the legs too.

RANK. Hm!—   190

NORA. Why are you looking so critical? Don't you think they
will fit me?

RANK. I have no means of forming an opinion about that.

NORA. [*looks at him for a moment*] For shame! [*hits him lightly on
the ear with the stockings*] That's to punish you. [*folds them up again*]

RANK. And what other nice things am I to be allowed to see?

NORA. Not a single thing more, for being so naughty. [*She looks* 195
among the things, humming to herself.]

RANK. [*after a short silence*] When I am sitting here, talking to
you as intimately as this, I cannot imagine for a moment what would
have become of me if I had never come into this house.

NORA. [*smiling*] I believe you do feel thoroughly at home
with us.

RANK. [*in a lower voice, looking straight in front of him*] And to be
obliged to leave it all—

NORA. Nonsense, you are not going to leave it.

RANK. [*as before*] And not be able to leave behind one the slight- 200
est token of one's gratitude, scarcely even a fleeting regret—nothing
but an empty place which the first comer can fill as well as any other.

NORA. And if I asked you now for a—? No!

RANK. For what?

NORA. For a big proof of your friendship—

RANK. Yes, yes!

NORA. I mean a tremendously big favour—   205

RANK. Would you really make me so happy for once?

NORA. Ah, but you don't know what it is yet.

RANK. No—but tell me.

NORA.   I really can't, Doctor Rank. It is something out of all reason; it means advice, and help, and a favour—

RANK.   The bigger a thing it is the better. I can't conceive what it is you mean. Do tell me. Haven't I your confidence?   210

NORA.   More than anyone else. I know you are my truest and best friend, and so I will tell you what it is. Well, Doctor Rank, it is something you must help me to prevent. You know how devotedly, how inexpressibly deeply Torvald loves me; he would never for a moment hesitate to give his life for me.

RANK.   [*leaning towards her*] Nora—do you think he is the only one—?

NORA.   [*with a slight start*] The only one—?

RANK.   The only one who would gladly give his life for your sake.

NORA.   [*sadly*] Is that it?   215

RANK.   I was determined you should know it before I went away, and there will never be a better opportunity than this. Now you know it, Nora. And now you know, too, that you can trust me as you would trust no one else.

NORA.   [*rises, deliberately and quietly*] Let me pass.

RANK.   [*makes room for her to pass him, but sits still*] Nora!

NORA.   [*at the hall door*] Helen, bring in the lamp. [*goes over to the stove*] Dear Doctor Rank, that was really horrid of you.

RANK.   To have loved you as much as anyone else does? Was that horrid?   220

NORA.   No, but to go and tell me so. There was really no need—

RANK.   What do you mean? Did you know—? [*MAID enters with lamp, puts it down on the table, and goes out.*] Nora—Mrs. Helmer—tell me, had you any idea of this?

NORA.   Oh, how do I know whether I had or whether I hadn't? I really can't tell you—To think you could be so clumsy, Doctor Rank! We were getting on so nicely.

RANK.   Well, at all events you know now that you can command me, body and soul. So won't you speak out?

NORA.   [*looking at him*] After what happened?   225

RANK.   I beg you to let me know what it is.

NORA.   I can't tell you anything now.

RANK.   Yes, yes. You mustn't punish me in that way. Let me have permission to do for you whatever a man may do.

NORA.   You can do nothing for me now. Besides, I really don't need any help at all. You will find that the whole thing is merely fancy on my part. It really is so—of course it is! [*Sits down in the rock-*

ing-chair, and looks at him with a smile] You are a nice sort of man, Doctor Rank!—don't you feel ashamed of yourself, now the lamp has come?

RANK.   Not a bit. But perhaps I had better go—for ever?   230

NORA.   No, indeed, you shall not. Of course you must come here just as before. You know very well Torvald can't do without you.

RANK.   Yes, but you?

NORA.   Oh, I am always tremendously pleased when you come.

RANK.   It is just that, that put me on the wrong track. You are a riddle to me. I have often thought that you would almost as soon be in my company as in Helmer's.

NORA.   Yes—you see there are some people one loves best, and   235 others whom one would almost always rather have as companions.

RANK.   Yes, there is something in that.

NORA.   When I was at home, of course I loved papa best. But I always thought it tremendous fun if I could steal down into the maid's room, because they never moralised at all, and talked to each other about such entertaining things.

RANK.   I see—it is *their* place I have taken.

NORA.   [*jumping up and going to him*] Oh, dear, nice Doctor Rank, I never meant that at all. But surely you can understand that being with Torvald is a little like being with papa—

[*Enter* MAID *from the hall*]

MAID.   If you please, ma'am. [*whispers and hands her a card*]   240

NORA.   [*glancing at the card*] Oh! [*puts it in her pocket*]

RANK.   Is there anything wrong?

NORA.   No, no, not in the least. It is only something—it is my new dress—

RANK.   What? Your dress is lying there.

NORA.   Oh, yes, that one; but this is another. I ordered it. Torvald   245 mustn't know about it—

RANK.   Oho! Then that was the great secret.

NORA.   Of course. Just go in to him; he is sitting in the inner room. Keep him as long as—

RANK.   Make your mind easy; I won't let him escape. [*goes into* HELMER'S *room*]

NORA.   [*to the* MAID] And he is standing waiting in the kitchen?

MAID.   Yes; he came up the back stairs.   250

NORA.   But didn't you tell him no one was in?

MAID.   Yes, but it was no good.

Nora. He won't go away?

Maid. No; he says he won't until he has seen you, ma'am.

Nora. Well, let him come in—but quietly. Helen, you mustn't say anything about it to anyone. It is a surprise for my husband.

Maid. Yes, ma'am, I quite understand. [*Exit.*]

Nora. This dreadful thing is going to happen! It will happen in spite of me! No, no, no, it can't happen—it shan't happen!

[*She bolts the door of* Helmer's *room. The* Maid *opens the hall door for* Krogstad *and shuts it after him. He is wearing a fur coat, high boots and a fur cap.*]

Nora. [*advancing towards him*] Speak low—my husband is at home.

Krogstad. No matter about that.

Nora. What do you want of me?   260

Krogstad. An explanation of something.

Nora. Make haste then. What is it?

Krogstad. You know, I suppose, that I have got my dismissal.

Nora. I couldn't prevent it, Mr. Krogstad. I fought as hard as I could on your side, but it was no good.

Krogstad. Does your husband love you so little, then? He   265 knows that what I can expose you to, and yet he ventures—

Nora. How can you suppose that he has any knowledge of the sort?

Krogstad. I didn't suppose so at all. It would not be the least like our dear Torvald Helmer to show so much courage—

Nora. Mr. Krogstad, a little respect for my husband, please.

Krogstad. Certainly—all the respect he deserves. But since you have kept the matter so carefully to yourself, I make bold to suppose that you have a little clearer idea, than you had yesterday, of what it actually is that you have done?

Nora. More than you could ever teach me.   270

Krogstad. Yes, such a bad lawyer as I am.

Nora. What is it you want of me?

Krogstad. Only to see how you were, Mrs. Helmer. I have been thinking about you all day long. A mere cashier, a quill-driver, a— well, a man like me—even he has a little of what is called feeling, you know.

Nora. Show it, then; think of my little children.

Krogstad. Have you and your husband thought of mine? But   275 never mind about that. I only wanted to tell you that you need not take this matter too seriously. In the first place there will be no accusation made on my part.

NORA. No, of course not; I was sure of that.

KROGSTAD. The whole thing can be arranged amicably; there is no reason why anyone should know anything about it. It will remain a secret between us three.

NORA. My husband must never get to know anything about it.

KROGSTAD. How will you be able to prevent it? Am I to understand that you can pay the balance that is owing?

NORA. No, not just at present.   280

KROGSTAD. Or perhaps that you have some expedient for raising the money soon?

NORA. No expedient that I mean to make use of.

KROGSTAD. Well, in any case, it would have been of no use to you now. If you stood there with ever so much money in your hand, I would never part with your bond.

NORA. Tell me what purpose you mean to put it to.

KROGSTAD. I shall only preserve it—keep it in my possession.   285 No one who is not concerned in the matter shall have the slightest hint of it. So that if the thought of it has driven you to any desperate resolution—

NORA. It has.

KROGSTAD. If you had it in your mind to run away from your home—

NORA. I had.

KROGSTAD. Or even something worse—

NORA. How could you know that?   290

KROGSTAD. Give up the idea.

NORA. How did you know I had thought of *that?*

KROGSTAD. Most of us think of that at first. I did, too—but I hadn't the courage.

NORA. [*faintly*] No more had I.

KROGSTAD. [*in a tone of relief*] No, that's it, isn't it—you hadn't 295 the courage either?

NORA. No, I haven't—I haven't.

KROGSTAD. Besides, it would have been a great piece of folly. Once the first storm at home is over—. I have a letter for your husband in my pocket.

NORA. Telling him everything?

KROGSTAD. In as lenient a manner as I possibly could.

NORA. [*quickly*] He mustn't get the letter. Tear it up. I will find 300 some means of getting money.

KROGSTAD.   Excuse me, Mrs. Helmer, but I think I told you just now—

NORA.   I am not speaking of what I owe you. Tell me what sum you are asking my husband for, and I will get the money.

KROGSTAD.   I am not asking your husband for a penny.

NORA.   What do you want, then?

KROGSTAD.   I will tell you. I want to rehabilitate myself, Mrs. 305 Helmer; I want to get on; and in that your husband must help me. For the last year and a half I have not had a hand in anything dishonourable, and all that time I have been struggling in most restricted circumstances. I was content to work my way up step by step. Now I am turned out, and I am not going to be satisfied with merely being taken into favour again. I want to get on, I tell you. I want to get into the Bank again, in a higher position. Your husband must make a place for me—

NORA.   That he will never do!

KROGSTAD.   He will; I know him; he dare not protest. And as soon as I am in there again with him, then you will see! Within a year I shall be the manager's right hand. It will be Nils Krogstad and not Torvald Helmer who manages the Bank.

NORA.   That's a thing you will never see!

KROGSTAD.   Do you mean that you will—?

NORA.   I have courage enough for it now.   310

KROGSTAD.   Oh, you can't frighten me. A fine, spoilt lady like you—

NORA.   You will see, you will see.

KROGSTAD.   Under the ice, perhaps? Down into the cold, coal-black water? And then, in the spring, to float up to the surface, all horrible and unrecognisable, with your hair fallen out—

NORA.   You can't frighten me.

KROGSTAD.   Nor you me. People don't do such things, Mrs. 315 Helmer. Besides, what use would it be? I should have him completely in my power all the same.

NORA.   Afterwards? When I am no longer—

KROGSTAD.   Have you forgotten that it is I who have the keeping of your reputation? [*NORA stands speechlessly looking at him.*] Well, now, I have warned you. Do not do anything foolish. When Helmer has had my letter, I shall expect a message from him. And be sure you remember that it is your husband himself who has forced me into such ways as this again. I will never forgive him for that. Good-bye, Mrs. Helmer.

[*Exit through the hall*]

NORA.   [*goes to the hall door, opens it slightly and listens*] He is going. He is not putting the letter in the box. Oh no, no! that's impossible! [*opens the door by degrees*] What is that? He is standing outside. He is not going downstairs. Is he hesitating? Can he—

[*A letter drops into the box; then* KROGSTAD'S *footsteps are heard, till they die away as he goes downstairs.* NORA *utters a stifled cry and runs across the room to the table by the sofa. A short pause.*]

NORA.   In the letter-box. [*steals across to the hall door*] There it lies—Torvald, Torvald, there is no hope for us now!

[MRS. LINDE *comes in from the room on the left, carrying the dress.*]

MRS. LINDE.   There, I can't see anything more to mend now.   320
Would you like to try it on—?
NORA.   [*in a hoarse whisper*] Christine, come here.
MRS. LINDE.   [*throwing the dress down on the sofa*] What is the matter with you? You look so agitated!
NORA.   Come here. Do you see that letter? There, look—you can see it through the glass in the letter-box.
MRS. LINDE.   Yes, I see it.
NORA.   That letter is from Krogstad.   325
MRS. LINDE.   Nora—it was Krogstad who lent you the money!
NORA.   Yes, and now Torvald will know all about it.
MRS. LINDE.   Believe me, Nora, that's the best thing for both of you.
NORA.   You don't know all. I forged a name.
MRS. LINDE.   Good heavens—!   330
NORA.   I only want to say this to you, Christine—you must be my witness.
MRS. LINDE.   Your witness? What do you mean? What am I to—?
NORA.   If I should go out of my mind—and it might easily happen—
MRS. LINDE.   Nora!
NORA.   Or if anything else should happen to me—anything, for   335
instance, that might prevent my being here—
MRS. LINDE.   Nora! Nora! you are quite out of your mind.
NORA.   And if it should happen that there were someone who wanted to take all the responsibility, all the blame, you understand—
MRS. LINDE.   Yes, yes—but how can you suppose—?

NORA.   Then you must be my witness, that it is not true, Christine. I am not out of my mind at all; I am in my right senses now, and I tell you no one else has known anything about it; I, and I alone, did the whole thing. Remember that.

MRS. LINDE.   I will, indeed. But I don't understand all this.   340

NORA.   How should you understand it? A wonderful thing is going to happen.

MRS. LINDE.   A wonderful thing?

NORA.   Yes, a wonderful thing!—But it is so terrible, Christine; it *mustn't* happen, not for all the world.

MRS. LINDE.   I will go at once and see Krogstad.

NORA.   Don't go to him; he will do you some harm.   345

MRS. LINDE.   There was a time when he would gladly do anything for my sake.

NORA.   He?

MRS. LINDE.   Where does he live?

NORA.   How should I know—? Yes [*feeling in her pocket*] here is his card. But the letter, the letter—!

HELMER.   [*calls from his room, knocking at the door*] Nora!   350

NORA.   [*cries out anxiously*] Oh, what's that? What do you want?

HELMER.   Don't be so frightened. We are not coming in; you have locked the door. Are you trying on your dress?

NORA.   Yes, that's it. I look so nice, Torvald.

MRS. LINDE.   [*who has read the card*] I see he lives at the corner here.

NORA.   Yes, but it's no use. It is hopeless. The letter is lying there   355 in the box.

MRS. LINDE.   And your husband keeps the key?

NORA.   Yes, always.

MRS. LINDE.   Krogstad must ask for his letter back unread, he must find some pretence—

NORA.   But it is just at this time that Torvald generally—

MRS. LINDE.   You must delay him. Go in to him in the meantime.   360 I will come back as soon as I can.

[*She goes out hurriedly through the hall door.*]

NORA.   [*goes to* HELMER'S *door, opens it and peeps in*] Torvald!

HELMER.   [*from the inner room*] Well? May I venture at last to come into my own room again? Come along, Rank, now you will see—[*halting in the doorway*] But what is this?

NORA.   What is what, dear?

HELMER.   Rank led me to expect a splendid transformation.

RANK. [*in the doorway*] I understood so, but evidently I was mis- 365
taken.

NORA. Yes, nobody is to have the chance of admiring me in my
dress until tomorrow.

HELMER. But, my dear Nora, you look so worn out. Have you
been practising too much?

NORA. No, I have not practised at all.

HELMER. But you will need to—

NORA. Yes, indeed I shall, Torvald. But I can't get on a bit with- 370
out you to help me; I have absolutely forgotten the whole thing.

HELMER. Oh, we will soon work it up again.

NORA. Yes, help me, Torvald. Promise that you will! I am so
nervous about it—all the people—. You must give yourself up to me
entirely this evening. Not the tiniest bit of business—you mustn't
even take a pen in your hand. Will you promise, Torvald dear?

HELMER. I promise. This evening I will be wholly and
absolutely at your service, you helpless little mortal. Ah, by the way,
first of all I will just—

[*Goes towards the hall door*]

NORA. What are you going to do there?

HELMER. Only see if any letters have come. 375

NORA. No, no! don't do that, Torvald!

HELMER. Why not?

NORA. Torvald, please don't. There is nothing there.

HELMER. Well, let me look. [*Turns to go to the letter-box. NORA, at
the piano, plays the first bars of the Tarantella. HELMER stops in the doorway.*] Aha!

NORA. I can't dance to-morrow if I don't practise with 380
you.

HELMER. [*going up to her*] Are you really so afraid of it, dear.

NORA. Yes, so dreadfully afraid of it. Let me practise at once;
there is time now, before we go to dinner. Sit down and play for me,
Torvald dear; criticise me, and correct me as you play.

HELMER. With great pleasure, if you wish me to.

[*Sits down at the piano.*]

NORA. [*takes out of the box a tambourine and a long variegated
shawl. She hastily drapes the shawl round her. Then she springs to the front
of the stage and calls out.*] Now play for me! I am going to dance!

[*HELMER plays and NORA dances. RANK stands by the piano behind HELMER and looks on.*]

HELMER.   [*as he plays*] Slower, slower!   385
NORA.   I can't do it any other way.
HELMER.   Not so violently, Nora!
NORA.   This is the way.
HELMER.   [*stops playing*] No, no—that is not a bit right.
NORA.   [*laughing and swinging the tambourine*] Didn't I tell you so?   390
RANK.   Let me play for her.
HELMER.   [*getting up*] Yes, do. I can correct her better then.

[*RANK sits down at the piano and plays. NORA dances more and more wildly. HELMER has taken up a position beside the stove, and during her dance gives her frequent instructions. She does not seem to hear him; her hair comes down and falls over her shoulders; she pays no attention to it, but goes on dancing. Enter MRS. LINDE.*]

MRS. LINDE.   [*standing as if spell-bound in the doorway*] Oh!—
NORA.   [*as she dances*] Such fun, Christine!
HELMER.   My dear darling Nora, you are dancing as if your life   395
depended on it.
NORA.   So it does.
HELMER.   Stop, Rank; this is sheer madness. Stop, I tell you!
[*RANK stops playing, and NORA suddenly stands still. HELMER goes up to her.*] I could never have believed it. You have forgotten everything I taught you.
NORA.   [*throwing away the tambourine*] There, you see.
HELMER.   You will want a lot of coaching.
NORA.   Yes, you see how much I need it. You must coach me up   400
to the last minute. Promise me that, Torvald!
HELMER.   You can depend on me.
NORA.   You must not think of anything but me, either to-day
or to-morrow; you mustn't open a single letter—not even open the
letter-box—
HELMER.   Ah, you are still afraid of that fellow—
NORA.   Yes, indeed I am.
HELMER.   Nora, I can tell from your looks that there is a letter   405
from him lying there.
NORA.   I don't know; I think there is; but you must not read anything of that kind now. Nothing horrid must come between us till
this is all over.

RANK. [*whispers to* HELMER] You mustn't contradict her.

HELMER. [*taking her in his arms*] The child shall have her way. But to-morrow night, after you have danced—

NORA. Then you will be free.

[MAID *appears in the doorway to the right.*]

MAID. Dinner is served, ma'am.   410

NORA. We will have champagne, Helen.

MAID. Very good, ma'am.   [*Exit.*]

HELMER. Hullo!—are we going to have a banquet?

NORA. Yes, a champagne banquet till the small hours. [*calls out*] And a few macaroons, Helen—lots, just for once!

HELMER. Come, come, don't be so wild and nervous. Be my   415 own little skylark, as you used.

NORA. Yes, dear, I will. But go in now and you too, Doctor Rank. Christine, you must help me to do up my hair.

RANK. [*whispers to* HELMER *s they go out*] I suppose there is nothing—she is not expecting anything?

HELMER. Far from it, my dear fellow; it is simply nothing more than this childish nervousness I was telling you of.

[*They go into the right-hand room.*]

NORA. Well!

MRS. LINDE. Gone out of town.   420

NORA. I could tell from your face.

MRS. LINDE. He is coming home to-morrow evening. I wrote a note for him.

NORA. You should have let it alone; you must prevent nothing. After all, it is splendid to be waiting for a wonderful thing to happen.

MRS. LINDE. What is it that you are waiting for?

NORA. Oh, you wouldn't understand. Go in to them, I will   425 come in a moment. [MRS. LINDE *goes into the dining-room.* NORA *stands still for a little while, as if to compose herself. Then she looks at her watch.*] Five o'clock. Seven hours till midnight; and then four-and-twenty hours till the next midnight. Then the Tarantella will be over. Twenty-four and seven? Thirty-one hours to live.

HELMER. [*from the doorway on the right*] Where's my little skylark?

NORA. [*going to him with her arms outstretched*] Here she is!

Act 3

THE SAME SCENE. *The table has been placed in the middle of the stage, with chairs round it. A lamp is burning on the table. The door into the hall stands open. Dance music is heard in the room above. MRS. LINDE is sitting at the table idly turning over the leaves of a book; she tries to read, but does not seem able to collect her thoughts. Every now and then she listens intently for a sound at the outer door.*

MRS. LINDE. [*looking at her watch*] Not yet—and the time is nearly up. If only he does not—. [*listens again*] Ah, there he is. [*Goes into the hall and opens the outer door carefully. Light footsteps are heard on the stairs. She whispers.*] Come in. There is no one here.

KROGSTAD. [*in the doorway*] I found a note from you at home. What does this mean?

MRS. LINDE. It is absolutely necessary that I should have a talk with you.

KROGSTAD. Really? And is it absolutely necessary that it should be here?

MRS. LINDE. It is impossible where I live; there is no private 5 entrance to my rooms. Come in; we are quite alone. The maid is asleep, and the Helmers are at the dance upstairs.

KROGSTAD. [*coming into the room*] Are the Helmers really at a dance to-night?

MRS. LINDE. Yes, why not?

KROGSTAD. Certainly—why not?

MRS. LINDE. Now, Nils, let us have a talk.

KROGSTAD. Can we two have anything to talk about? 10

MRS. LINDE. We have a great deal to talk about.

KROGSTAD. I shouldn't have thought so.

MRS. LINDE. No, you have never properly understood me.

KROGSTAD. Was there anything else to understand except what was obvious to all the world—a heartless woman jilts a man when a more lucrative chance turns up?

MRS. LINDE. Do you believe I am as absolutely heartless as all 15 that? And do you believe that I did it with a light heart?

KROGSTAD. Didn't you?

MRS. LINDE. Nils, did you really think that?

KROGSTAD. If it were as you say, why did you write to me as you did at the time?

MRS. LINDE. I could do nothing else. As I had to break with you, it was my duty also to put an end to all that you felt for me.

KROGSTAD. [*wringing his hands*] So that was it. and all this—only 20 for the sake of money!

Mrs. Linde.   You must not forget that I had a helpless mother and two little brothers. We couldn't wait for you, Nils; your prospects seemed hopeless then.

Krogstad.   That may be so, but you had no right to throw me over for any one else's sake.

Mrs. Linde.   Indeed I don't know. Many a time did I ask myself if I had the right to do it.

Krogstad.   [*more gently*] When I lost you, it was as if all the solid ground went from under my feet. Look at me now—I am a ship-wrecked man clinging to a bit of wreckage.

Mrs. Linde.   But help may be near.   25

Krogstad.   *It was* near; but then you came and stood in my way.

Mrs. Linde.   Unintentionally, Nils. It was only to-day that I learnt it was your place I was going to take in the Bank.

Krogstad.   I believe you, if you say so. But now that you know it, are you not going to give it up to me?

Mrs. Linde.   No, because that would not benefit you in the least.

Krogstad.   Oh, benefit, benefit—I would have done it whether   30
or no.

Mrs. Linde.   I have learnt to act prudently. Life, and hard, bitter necessity have taught me that.

Krogstad.   And life has taught me not to believe in fine speeches.

Mrs. Linde.   Then life has taught you something very reasonable. But deeds you must believe in?

Krogstad.   What do you mean by that?

Mrs. Linde.   You said you were like a shipwrecked man cling-   35
ing to some wreckage.

Krogstad.   I had good reason to say so.

Mrs. Linde.   Well, I am like a shipwrecked woman clinging to some wreckage—no one to mourn for, no one to care for.

Krogstad.   It was your own choice.

Mrs. Linde.   There was no other choice—then.

Krogstad.   Well, what now?   40

Mrs. Linde.   Nils, how would it be if we two shipwrecked people could join forces?

Krogstad.   What are you saying?

Mrs. Linde.   Two on the same piece of wreckage would stand a better chance than each on their own.

Krogstad.   Christine!

Mrs. Linde.   What do you suppose brought me to town?   45

Krogstad.   Do you mean that you gave me a thought?

MRS. LINDE. I could not endure life without work. All my life, as long as I can remember, I have worked, and it has been my greatest and only pleasure. But now I am quite alone in the world—my life is so dreadfully empty and I feel so forsaken. There is not the least pleasure in working for one's self. Nils, give me someone and something to work for.

KROGSTAD. I don't trust that. It is nothing but a woman's overstrained sense of generosity that prompts you to make such an offer of yourself.

MRS. LINDE. Have you ever noticed anything of the sort in me?

KROGSTAD. Could you really do it? Tell me—do you know all about my past life?

MRS. LINDE. Yes.

KROGSTAD. And do you know what they think of me here?

MRS. LINDE. You seemed to me to imply that with me you might have been quite another man.

KROGSTAD. I am certain of it.

MRS. LINDE. Is it too late now?

KROGSTAD. Christine, are you saying this deliberately? Yes, I am sure you are. I see it in your face. Have you really the courage, then—?

MRS. LINDE. I want to be a mother to someone, and your children need a mother. We two need each other. Nils, I have faith in your real character—I can dare anything together with you.

KROGSTAD. [*grasps her hands*] Thanks, thanks, Christine! Now I shall find a way to clear myself in the eyes of the world. Ah, but I forgot—

MRS. LINDE. [*listening*] Hush! The Tarantella! Go, go!

KROGSTAD. Why? What is it?

MRS. LINDE. Do you hear them up there? When that is over, we may expect them back.

KROGSTAD. Yes, yes—I will go. But it is all no use. Of course you are not aware what steps I have taken in the matter of the Helmers.

MRS. LINDE. Yes. I know all about that.

KROGSTAD. And in spite of that have you the courage to—?

MRS. LINDE. I understand very well to what lengths a man like you might be driven by despair.

KROGSTAD. If I could only undo what I have done!

MRS. LINDE. You can. Your letter is lying in the letter-box now.

KROGSTAD. Are you sure of that?

MRS. LINDE. Quite sure, but—

KROGSTAD.   [*with a searching look at her*] Is that what it all   70
means?—that you want to save your friend at any cost? Tell me
frankly. Is that it?

MRS. LINDE.   Nils, a woman who has once sold herself for
another's sake, doesn't do it a second time.

KROGSTAD.   I will ask for my letter back.

MRS. LINDE.   No, no.

KROGSTAD.   Yes, of course I will. I will wait here till Helmer
comes; I will tell him he must give me my letter back—that it only
concerns my dismissal—that he is not to read it—

MRS. LINDE.   No, Nils, you must not recall your letter.   75

KROGSTAD.   But, tell me, wasn't it for that very purpose that you
asked me to meet you here?

MRS. LINDE.   In my first moment of fright, it was. But twenty-
four hours have elapsed since then, and in that time I have witnessed
incredible things in this house. Helmer must know all about it. This
unhappy secret must be disclosed; they must have a complete understanding between them, which is impossible with all this conceal-
ment and falsehood going on.

KROGSTAD.   Very well, if you will take the responsibility. But
there is one thing I can do in any case, and I shall do it at once.

MRS. LINDE.   [*listening*] You must be quick and go! The dance is
over; we are not safe a moment longer.

KROGSTAD.   I will wait for you below.   80

MRS. LINDE.   Yes, do. You must see me back to my door.

KROGSTAD.   I have never had such an amazing piece of good for-
tune in my life.

[*Goes out through the outer door. The door between the room and the hall
remains open.*]

MRS. LINDE.   [*tidying up the room and laying her hat and cloak ready*]
What a difference! what a difference! Someone to work for and live
for—a home to bring comfort into. That I will do, indeed. I wish they
would be quick and come—[*listens*] Ah, there they are now. I must
put on my things.

[*Takes up her hat and cloak. HELMER'S and NORA'S voices are heard outside;
a key is turned, and HELMER brings NORA almost by force into the hall. She
is in an Italian costume with a large black shawl round her; he is in evening
dress and a black domino which is flying open.*]

NORA. [*hanging back in the doorway, and struggling with him*] No, no, no!—don't take me in. I want to go upstairs again; I don't want to leave so early.

HELMER.   But, my dearest Nora—   85

NORA.   Please, Torvald dear—please, *please*—only an hour more.

HELMER.   Not a single minute, my sweet Nora. You know that was our agreement. Come along into the room; you are catching cold standing there.

[*He brings her gently into the room, in spite of her resistance.*]

MRS. LINDE.   Good evening.

NORA.   Christine!

HELMER.   You here, so late, Mrs. Linde?   90

MRS. LINDE.   Yes, you must excuse me; I was so anxious to see Nora in her dress.

NORA.   Have you been sitting here waiting for me?

MRS. LINDE.   Yes, unfortunately I came too late, you had already gone upstairs; and I thought I couldn't go away without having seen you.

HELMER.   [*taking off NORA'S shawl*] Yes, take a good look at her. I think she is worth looking at. Isn't she charming, Mrs. Linde?

MRS. LINDE.   Yes, indeed she is.   95

HELMER.   Doesn't she look remarkably pretty? Everyone thought so at the dance. But she is terribly self-willed, this sweet little person. What are we to do with her? You will hardly believe that I had almost to bring her away by force.

NORA.   Torvald, you will repent not having let me stay, even if it were only for half an hour.

HELMER.   Listen to her, Mrs. Linde! She had danced her Tarantella, and it had been a tremendous success, as it deserved—although possibly the performance was a trifle too realistic—a little more so, I mean, than was strictly compatible with the limitations of art. But never mind about that! The chief thing is, she had made a success—she had made a tremendous success. Do you think I was going to let her remain there after that, and spoil the effect? No indeed! I took my charming little Capri maiden—my capricious little Capri maiden, I should say—on my arm; took one quick turn round the room; a curtsey on either side, and, as they say in novels, the beautiful apparition disappeared. An exit ought always to be effective, Mrs. Linde; but that is what I cannot make Nora understand. Pooh! this room is hot. [*throws his domino on a chair and opens the door of his room*] Hullo! it's all dark in here. Oh, of course—excuse me—.

[*He goes in and lights some candles.*]

NORA.   [*in a hurried and breathless whisper*] Well?
MRS. LINDE.   [*in a low voice*] I have had a talk with him.   100
NORA.   Yes, and—
MRS. LINDE.   Nora, you must tell your husband all about it.
NORA.   [*in an expressionless voice*] I knew it.
MRS. LINDE.   You have nothing to be afraid of as far as Krogstad is concerned; but you must tell him.
NORA.   I won't tell him.   105
MRS. LINDE.   Then the letter will.
NORA.   Thank you, Christine. Now I know what I must do. Hush—!
HELMER.   [*coming in again*] Well, Mrs. Linde, have you admired her?
MRS. LINDE.   Yes, and now I will say good-night.
HELMER.   What already? Is this yours, this knitting?   110
MRS. LINDE.   [*taking it*] Yes, thank you, I had very nearly forgotten it.
HELMER.   So you knit?
MRS. LINDE.   Of course.
HELMER.   Do you know, you ought to embroider.
MRS. LINDE.   Really? Why?   115
HELMER.   Yes, it's far more becoming. Let me show you. You hold the embroidery thus in your left hand, and use the needle with the right—like this—with a long, easy sweep. Do you see?
MRS. LINDE.   Yes, perhaps—
HELMER.   But in the case of knitting—that can never be anything but ungraceful; look here—the arms close together, the knitting-needles going up and down—it has a sort of Chinese effect—. That was really excellent champagne they gave us.
MRS. LINDE.   Well,—good-night, Nora, and don't be self-willed any more.
HELMER.   That's right, Mrs. Linde.   120
MRS. LINDE.   Good-night, Mr. Helmer.
HELMER.   [*accompanying her to the door*] Good-night, good-night. I hope you will get home all right. I should be very happy to—but you haven't any great distance to go. Good-night, good-night. [*She

goes out; he shuts the door after her, and comes in again.] Ah!—at last we have got rid of her. She is a frightful bore, that woman.

NORA.   Aren't you very tired, Torvald?

HELMER.   No, not in the least.

NORA.   Nor sleepy?   125

HELMER.   Not a bit. On the contrary, I feel extraordinarily lively. And you?—you really look both tired and sleepy.

NORA.   Yes, I am very tired. I want to go to sleep at once.

HELMER.   There, you see it was quite right of me not to let you stay there any longer.

NORA.   Everything you do is quite right, Torvald.

HELMER.   [*kissing her on the forehead*] Now my little skylark is   130 speaking reasonably. Did you notice what good spirits Rank was in this evening?

NORA.   Really? Was he? I didn't speak to him at all.

HELMER.   And I very little, but I have not for a long time seen him in such good form. [*looks for a while at her and then goes nearer to her*] It is delightful to be at home by ourselves again, to be all alone with you—you fascinating, charming little darling!

NORA.   Don't look at me like that, Torvald.

HELMER.   Why shouldn't I look at my dearest treasure?—at all the beauty that is mine, all my very own?

NORA.   [*going to the other side of the table*] You mustn't say things   135 like that to me to-night.

HELMER.   [*following her*] You have still got the Tarantella in your blood, I see. And it makes you more captivating than ever. Listen— the guests are beginning to go now. [*in a lower voice*] Nora—soon the whole house will be quiet.

NORA.   Yes, I hope so.

HELMER.   Yes, my own darling Nora. Do you know, when I am out at a party with you like this, why I speak so little to you, keep away from you, and only send a stolen glance in your direction now and then?—do you know why I do that? It is because I make believe to myself that we are secretly in love, and you are my secretly promised bride, and that no one suspects there is anything between us.

NORA.   Yes, yes—I know very well your thoughts are with me all the time.

HELMER.   And when we are leaving, and I am putting the shawl   140 over your beautiful young shoulders—on your lovely neck—then I imagine that you are my young bride and that we have just come from the wedding, and I am bringing you for the first time into our home—to be alone with you for the first time—quite alone with my shy little darling! All this evening I have longed for nothing but you. When I watched the seductive figures of the Tarantella, my blood was on fire; I could endure it no longer, and that was why I brought you down so early—

NORA.   Go away, Torvald! You must let me go. I won't—

HELMER.   What's that? You're joking, my little Nora! You won't—you won't? Am I not your husband—?

[*A knock is heard at the outer door.*]

NORA.   [*starting*] Did you hear—?

HELMER.   [*going into the hall*] Who is it?

RANK.   [*outside*] It is I. May I come in for a moment?   145

HELMER.   [*in a fretful whisper*] Oh, what does he want now? [*aloud*] Wait a minute! [*unlocks the door*] Come, that's kind of you not to pass by our door.

RANK.   I thought I heard your voice, and felt as if I should like to look in. [*with a swift glance round*] Ah, yes!—these dear familiar rooms. You are very happy and cosy in here, you two.

HELMER.   It seems to me that you looked after yourself pretty well upstairs too.

RANK.   Excellently. Why shouldn't I? Why shouldn't one enjoy everything in this world?—at any rate as much as one can, and as long as one can. The wine was capital—

HELMER.   Especially the champagne.   150

RANK.   So you noticed that too? It is almost incredible how much I managed to put away!

NORA.   Torvald drank a great deal of champagne tonight, too.

RANK.   Did he?

NORA.   Yes, and he is always in such good spirits afterwards.

RANK.   Well, why should one not enjoy a merry evening after a   155 well-spent day?

HELMER.   Well spent? I am afraid I can't take credit for that.

RANK.   [*clapping him on the back*] But I can, you know!

NORA.   Doctor Rank, you must have been occupied with some scientific investigation to-day.

RANK.   Exactly.

HELMER.   Just listen!—little Nora talking about scientific   160 investigations!

NORA.   And may I congratulate you on the result?

RANK.   Indeed you may.

NORA. Was it favourable, then?

RANK. The best possible, for both doctor and patient—certainty.

NORA. [*quickly and searchingly*] Certainty?   165

RANK. Absolute certainty. So wasn't I entitled to make a merry evening of it after that?

NORA. Yes, you certainly were, Doctor Rank.

HELMER. I think so too, so long as you don't have to pay for it in the morning.

RANK. Oh well, one can't have anything in this life without paying for it.

NORA. Doctor Rank—are you fond of fancy-dress balls?   170

RANK. Yes, if there is a fine lot of pretty costumes.

NORA. Tell me—what shall we two wear at the next?

HELMER. Little featherbrain!—are you thinking of the next already?

RANK. We two? Yes, I can tell you. You shall go as a good fairy—

HELMER. Yes, but what do you suggest as an appropriate cos-   175
tume for that?

RANK. Let your wife go dressed just as she is in everyday life.

HELMER. That was really very prettily turned. But can't you tell us what you will be?

RANK. Yes, my dear friend, I have quite made up my mind about that.

HELMER. Well?

RANK. At the next fancy dress ball I shall be invisible.   180

HELMER. That's a good joke!

RANK. There is a big black hat—have you never heard of hats that make you invisible? If you put one on, no one can see you.

HELMER. [*suppressing a smile*] Yes, you are quite right.

RANK. But I am clean forgetting what I came for. Helmer, give me a cigar—one of the dark Havanas.

HELMER. With the greatest pleasure. [*offers him his case*]   185

RANK. [*takes a cigar and cuts off the end*] Thanks.

NORA. [*striking a match*] Let me give you a light.

RANK. Thank you. [*She holds the match for him to light his cigar.*] And now good-bye!

HELMER. Good-bye, good-bye, dear old man!

NORA. Sleep well, Doctor Rank.   190

RANK. Thank you for that wish.

NORA. Wish me the same.

RANK. You? Well, if you want me to sleep well! And thanks for the light.

[*He nods to them both and goes out.*]

HELMER.   [*in a subdued voice*] He has drunk more than he ought.

NORA.   [*absently*] Maybe. [HELMER *takes a bunch of keys out of his* 195 *pocket and goes into the hall.*] Torvald! what are you going to do there?

HELMER.   Empty the letter-box; it is quite full; there will be no room to put the newspaper in to-morrow morning.

NORA.   Are you going to work to-night?

HELMER.   You know quite well I'm not. What is this? Some one has been at the lock.

NORA.   At the lock—?

HELMER.   Yes, someone has. What can it mean? I should never 200 have thought the maid—. Here is a broken hairpin. Nora, it is one of yours.

NORA.   [*quickly*] Then it must have been the children—

HELMER.   Then you must get them out of those ways. There, at last I have got it open. [*Takes out the contents of the letter-box, and calls to the kitchen.*] Helen!—Helen, put out the light over the front door. [*Goes back into the room and shuts the door into the hall. He holds out his hand full of letters.*] Look at that—look what a heap of them there are. [*turning them over*] What on earth is that?

NORA.   [*at the window*] The letter—No! Torvald, no!

HELMER.   Two cards—of Rank's.

NORA.   Of Doctor Rank's?   205

HELMER.   [*looking at them*] Doctor Rank. They were on the top. He must have put them in when he went out.

NORA.   Is there anything written on them?

HELMER.   There is a black cross over the name. Look there— what an uncomfortable idea! It looks as if he were announcing his own death.

NORA.   It is just what he is doing.

HELMER.   What? Do you know anything about it? Has he said 210 anything to you?

NORA.   Yes. He told me that when the cards came it would be his leave-taking from us. He means to shut himself up and die.

HELMER.   My poor old friend. Certainly I knew we should not have him very long with us. But so soon! And so he hides himself away like a wounded animal.

NORA.   If it has to happen, it is best it should be without a word—don't you think so, Torvald?

HELMER.   [*walking up and down*] He had so grown into our lives. I can't think of him as having gone out of them. He, with his sufferings and his loneliness, was like a cloudy background to our sunlit happiness. Well, perhaps it is best so. For him, anyway. [*standing still*] And perhaps for us too, Nora. We two are thrown quite upon each other now. [*puts his arms round her*] My darling wife, I don't feel as if I could hold you tight enough. Do you know, Nora, I have often wished that you might be threatened by some great danger, so that I might risk my life's blood, and everything, for your sake.

NORA. [*disengages herself, and says firmly and decidedly*] Now you   215 must read your letters, Torvald.

HELMER. No, no; not to-night. I want to be with you, my darling wife.

NORA. With the thought of your friend's death—

HELMER. You are right, it has affected us both. Something ugly has come between us—the thought of the horrors of death. We must try and rid our minds of that. Until then—we will each go to our own room.

NORA. [*hanging on his neck*] Good-night, Torvald—Good-night!

HELMER. [*kissing her on the forehead*]. Good-night, my little   220 singing-bird. Sleep sound, Nora. Now I will read my letters through.

[*He takes his letters and goes into his room, shutting the door after him.*]

NORA. [*gropes distractedly about, seizes* HELMER'S *domino, throws it round her, while she says in quick, hoarse, spasmodic whispers*] Never to see him again. Never! Never! [*puts her shawl over her head*] Never to see my children again either—never again. Never! Never!—Ah! the icy, black water—the unfathomable depths—If only it were over! He has got it now—now he is reading it. Good-by, Torvald and my children!

[*She is about to rush out through the hall, when* HELMER *opens his door hurriedly and stands with an open letter in his hand.*]

HELMER. Nora!

NORA. Ah!—

HELMER. What is this? Do you know what is in this letter?

NORA. Yes, I know. Let me go! Let me get out!   225

HELMER. [*holding her back*] Where are you going?

NORA. [*trying to get free*] You shan't save me, Torvald!

HELMER. [*reeling*] True? Is this true, that I read here? Horrible! No, no—it is impossible that it can be true.

NORA. It is true. I have loved you above everything else in the world.

HELMER. Oh, don't let us have any silly excuses.   230

NORA. [*taking a step towards him*] Torvald—!

HELMER.   Miserable creature—what have you done?

NORA.   Let me go. You shall not suffer for my sake. You shall not take it upon yourself.

HELMER.   No tragedy airs, please. [*locks the hall door*] Here you shall stay and give me an explanation. Do you understand what you have done? Answer me? Do you understand what you have done?

NORA.   [*looks steadily at him and says with a growing look of coldness* 235 *in her face*] Yes, now I am beginning to understand thoroughly.

HELMER.   [*walking about the room*] What a horrible awakening! All these eight years—she who was my joy and pride—a hypocrite, a liar—worse, worse—a criminal! The unutterable ugliness of it all! For shame! For shame! [*NORA is silent and looks steadily at him. He stops in front of her.*] I ought to have suspected that something of the sort would happen. I ought to have foreseen it. All your father's want of principle—be silent!—all your father's want of principle has come out in you. No religion, no morality, no sense of duty—. How I am punished for having winked at what he did! I did it for your sake, and this is how you repay me.

NORA.   Yes, that's just it.

HELMER.   Now you have destroyed all my happiness. You have ruined all my future. It is horrible to think of! I am in the power of an unscrupulous man; he can do what he likes with me, ask anything he likes of me, give me any orders he pleases—I dare not refuse. And I must sink to such miserable depths because of a thoughtless woman!

NORA.   When I am out of the way, you will be free.

HELMER.   No fine speeches, please. Your father had always 240 plenty of those ready, too. What good would it be to me if you were out of the way, as you say? Not the slightest. He can make the affair known everywhere; and if he does, I may be falsely suspected of having been a party to your criminal action. Very likely people will think I was behind it all—that it was I who prompted you! And I have to thank you for all this—you whom I have cherished during the whole of our married life. Do you understand now what it is you have done for me?

NORA.   [*coldly and quietly*] Yes.

HELMER.   It is so incredible that I can't take it in. But we must come to some understanding. Take off that shawl. Take it off, I tell you. I must try and appease him some way or another. The matter must be hushed up at any cost. And as for you and me, it must appear as if everything between us were just as before—but naturally only in the eyes of the world. You will still remain in my house, that is a matter of course. But I shall not allow you to bring up the children; I dare not trust them to you. To think that I should be obliged to say so to one whom I have loved so dearly, and whom I still—. No, that is all over. From this moment happiness is not the question; all that concerns us is to save the remains, the fragments, the appearance—

[*A ring is heard at the front-door bell.*]

HELMER. [*with a start*] What is that? So late! Can the worst—? Can he—? Hide yourself, Nora. Say you are ill.

[*NORA stands motionless. HELMER goes and unlocks the hall door.*]

MAID. [*half-dressed, comes to the door*] A letter for the mistress.

HELMER. Give it to me. [*takes the letter, and shuts the door*] Yes, it 245 is from him. You shall not have it; I will read it myself.

NORA. Yes, read it.

HELMER. [*standing by the lamp*] I scarcely have the courage to do it. It may mean ruin for both of us. No, I must know. [*tears open the letter, runs his eye over a few lines, looks at a paper enclosed and gives a shout of joy*] Nora! [*She looks at him questioningly.*] Nora!—No, I must read it once again—. Yes, it is true! I am saved! Nora, I am saved!

NORA. And I?

HELMER. You too, of course; we are both saved, both you and I. Look, he sends you your bond back. He says he regrets and repents— that a happy change in his life—never mind what he says! We are saved, Nora! No one can do anything to you. Oh, Nora, Nora!—no, first I must destroy these hateful things. Let me see—. [*takes a look at the bond*] No, no, I won't look at it. The whole thing shall be nothing but a bad dream to me. [*tears up the bond and both letters, throws them all into the stove, and watches them burn*] There—now it doesn't exist any longer. He says that since Christmas Eve you—. These must have been three dreadful days for you, Nora.

NORA. I have fought a hard fight these three days.   250

HELMER. And suffered agonies, and seen no way out but—. No, we won't call any of the horrors to mind. We will only shout with joy, and keep saying "It's all over! It's all over!" Listen to me, Nora. You don't seem to realise that it is all over. What is this?—such a cold, set face! My poor little Nora, I quite understand; you don't feel as if you could believe that I have forgiven you. But it is true, Nora, I swear it; I have forgiven you everything. I know that what you did, you did out of love for me.

NORA. That is true.

HELMER.   You have loved me as a wife ought to love her husband. Only you had not sufficient knowledge to judge of the means you used. But do you suppose you are any the less dear to me, because you don't understand how to act on your own responsibility? No, no; only lean on me; I will advise you and direct you. I should not be a man if this womanly helplessness did not just give you a double attractiveness in my eyes. You must not think any more about the hard things I said in my first moment of consternation, when I thought everything was going to overwhelm me. I have forgiven you, Nora; I swear to you I have forgiven you.

NORA.   Thank you for your forgiveness.

[*She goes out through the door to the right.*]

HELMER.   No, don't go—. [*looks in*] What are you doing in there?   255

NORA.   [*from within*] Taking off my fancy dress.

HELMER.   [*standing at the open door*] Yes, do. Try and calm yourself, and make your mind easy again, my frightened little singingbird. Be at rest, and feel secure; I have broad wings to shelter you under. [*walks up and down by the door*] How warm and cosy our home is, Nora. Here is shelter for you; here I will protect you like a hunted dove that I have saved from a hawk's claws. I will bring peace to your poor beating heart. It will come, little by little, Nora, believe me. Tomorrow morning you will look upon it all quite differently; soon everything will be just as it was before. Very soon you won't need me to assure you that I have forgiven you; you will yourself feel the certainty that I have done so. Can you suppose I should ever think of such a thing as repudiating you, or even reproaching you? You have no idea what a true man's heart is like, Nora. There is something so indescribably sweet and satisfying, to a man, in the knowledge that he has forgiven his wife—forgiven her freely, and with all his heart. It seems as if that had made her, as it were, doubly his own; he has given her a new life, so to speak; and she has in a way become both wife and child to him. So you shall be for me after this, my little scared, helpless darling. Have no anxiety about anything, Nora; only be frank and open with me, and I will serve as will and conscience both to you—. What is this? Not gone to bed? Have you changed your things?

NORA.   [*in everyday dress*] Yes, Torvald, I have changed my things now.

HELMER.   But what for?—so late as this.

NORA.   I shall not sleep to-night.   260

HELMER.   But, my dear Nora—

NORA.   [*looking at her watch*] It is not so very late. Sit down here, Torvald. You and I have much to say to one another.

[*She sits down at one side of the table.*]

HELMER.   Nora—what is this?—this cold, set face?

NORA.   Sit down. it will take some time; I have a lot to talk over with you.

HELMER.   [*sits down at the opposite side of the table*] You alarm me, Nora!—and I don't understand you.   265

NORA.   No, that is just it. You don't understand me, and I have never understood you either—before to-night. No, you mustn't interrupt me. You must simply listen to what I say. Torvald, this is a settling of accounts.

HELMER.   What do you mean by that?

NORA.   [*after a short silence*] Isn't there one thing that strikes you as strange in our sitting here like this?

HELMER.   What is that?

NORA.   We have been married now eight years. Does it not occur to you that this is the first time we two, you and I, husband and wife, have had a serious conversation?   270

HELMER.   What do you mean by serious?

NORA.   In all these eight years—longer than that—from the very beginning of our acquaintance, we have never exchanged a word on any serious subject.

HELMER.   Was it likely that I would be continually and for ever telling you about worries that you could not help me to bear?

NORA.   I am not speaking about business matters. I say that we have never sat down in earnest together to try and get at the bottom of anything.

HELMER.   But, dearest Nora, would it have been any good to you?   275

NORA.   That is just it; you have never understood me. I have been greatly wronged, Torvald—first by papa and then by you.

HELMER.   What! By us two—by us two, who have loved you better than anyone else in the world?

NORA.   [*shaking her head*] You have never loved me. You have only thought it pleasant to be in love with me.

HELMER.   Nora, what do I hear you saying?

NORA.   It is perfectly true, Torvald. When I was at home with papa, he told me his opinion about everything, and so I had the same opinions; and if I differed from him I concealed the fact, because he would not have liked it. He called me his doll-child, and he played with me just as I used to play with my dolls. And when I came to live with you—   280

HELMER. What sort of an expression is that to use about our marriage?

NORA. [*undisturbed*] I mean that I was simply transferred from papa's hands into yours. You arranged everything according to your own taste, and so I got the same tastes as you—or else I pretended to, I am really not quite sure which—I think sometimes the one and sometimes the other. When I look back on it, it seems to me as if I had been living here like a poor woman—just from hand to mouth. I have existed merely to perform tricks for you, Torvald. But you would have it so. You and papa have committed a great sin against me. It is your fault that I have made nothing of my life.

HELMER. How unreasonable and how ungrateful you are, Nora! Have you not been happy here?

NORA. No, I have never been happy. I thought I was, but it has never really been so.

HELMER. Not—not happy! 285

NORA. No, only merry. And you have always been so kind to me. But our home has been nothing but a playroom. I have been your doll-wife, just as at home I was papa's doll-child; and here the children have been my dolls. I thought it great fun when you played with me, just as they thought it great fun when I played with them. That is what our marriage has been, Torvald.

HELMER. There is some truth in what you say—exaggerated and strained as your view of it is. But for the future it shall be different. Playtime shall be over, and lesson-time shall begin.

NORA. Whose lessons? Mine, or the children's?

HELMER. Both yours and the children's, my darling Nora.

NORA. Alas, Torvald, you are not the man to educate me into 290 being a proper wife for you.

HELMER. And you can say that!

NORA. And I—how am I fitted to bring up the children?

HELMER. Nora!

NORA. Didn't you say so yourself a little while ago—that you dare not trust me to bring them up?

HELMER. In a moment of anger! Why do you pay any heed to 295 that?

NORA. Indeed, you were perfectly right. I am not fit for the task. There is another task I must undertake first. I must try and educate myself—you are not the man to help me in that. I must do that for myself. And that is why I am going to leave you now.

HELMER. [*springing up*] What do you say?

NORA. I must stand quite alone, if I am to understand myself and everything about me. It is for that reason that I cannot remain with you any longer.

HELMER Nora! Nora!

NORA. I am going away from here now, at once. I am sure Christine will take me in for the night—

HELMER. You are out of your mind! I won't allow it! I forbid you!

NORA. It is no use forbidding me anything any longer. I will take with me what belongs to myself. I will take nothing from you, either now or later.

HELMER. What sort of madness is this!

NORA. To-morrow I shall go home—I mean, to my old home. It will be easiest for me to find something to do there.

HELMER. You blind, foolish woman!

NORA. I must try and get some sense, Torvald.

HELMER. To desert your home, your husband and your children! And you don't consider what people will say!

NORA. I cannot consider that at all. I only know that it is necessary for me.

HELMER. It's shocking. This is how you would neglect your most sacred duties.

NORA. What do you consider my most sacred duties?

HELMER. Do I need to tell you that? Are they not your duties to your husband and your children?

NORA. I have other duties just as sacred.

HELMER. That you have not. What duties could those be?

NORA. Duties to myself.

HELMER. Before all else, you are a wife and a mother.

NORA. I don't believe that any longer. I believe that before all else I am a reasonable human being, just as you are—or, at all events, that I must try and become one. I know quite well, Torvald, that most people would think you right, and that views of that kind are to be found in books; but I can no longer content myself with what most people say, or with what is found in books. I must think over things for myself and get to understand them.

HELMER. Can you not understand your place in your own home? Have you not a reliable guide in such matters as that?—have you no religion?

NORA. I am afraid, Torvald, I do not exactly know what religion is.

HELMER.   What are you saying?

NORA.   I know nothing but what the clergyman said when I   320
went to be confirmed. He told us that religion was this, and that, and
the other. When I am away from all this, and am alone, I will look
into that matter too. I will see if what the clergyman said is true, or at
all events if it is true for me.

HELMER.   This is unheard of in a girl of your age! But if religion
cannot lead you aright, let me try and awaken your conscience. I suppose you have some moral sense? Or—answer me—am I to think
you have none?

NORA.   I assure you, Torvald, that is not an easy question to
answer. I really don't know. The thing perplexes me altogether. I only
know that you and I look at it in quite a different light. I am learning,
too, that the law is quite another thing from what I supposed; but I
find it impossible to convince myself that the law is right. According
to it a woman has no right to spare her old dying father, or to save
her husband's life. I can't believe that.

HELMER.   You talk like a child. You don't understand the conditions of the world in which you live.

NORA.   No, I don't. But now I am going to try. I am going to see
if I can make out who is right, the world or I.

HELMER.   You are ill, Nora; you are delirious; I almost think you   325
are out of your mind.

NORA.   I have never felt my mind so clear and certain as
to-night.

HELMER.   And is it with a clear and certain mind that you for-
sake your husband and your children?

NORA.   Yes, it is.

HELMER.   Then there is only one possible explanation.

NORA.   What is that?   330

HELMER.   You do not love me any more.

NORA.   No, that is just it.

HELMER.   Nora!—and you can say that?

NORA.   It gives me great pain, Torvald, for you have always
been so kind to me, but I cannot help it. I do not love you any more.

HELMER.   [regaining his composure] Is that a clear and certain con-   335
viction too?

NORA.   Yes, absolutely clear and certain. That is the reason why
I will not stay here any longer.

HELMER.   And can you tell me what I have done to forfeit your
love?

NORA. Yes, indeed I can. It was to-night, when the wonderful thing did not happen; then I saw you were not the man I had thought you.

HELMER. Explain yourself better—I don't understand you.

NORA. I have waited so patiently for eight years; for, goodness 340 knows, I knew very well that wonderful things don't happen every day. Then this horrible misfortune came upon me; and then I felt quite certain that the wonderful thing was going to happen at last. When Krogstad's letter was lying out there, never for a moment did I imagine that you would consent to accept this man's conditions. I was so absolutely certain that you would say to him: Publish the thing to the whole world. And when that was done—

HELMER. Yes, what then?—when I had exposed my wife to shame and disgrace?

NORA. When that was done, I was so absolutely certain, you would come forward and take everything upon yourself, and say: I am the guilty one.

HELMER. Nora—!

NORA. You mean that I would never have accepted such a sacrifice on your part? No, of course not. But what would my assurances have been worth against yours? That was the wonderful thing which I hoped for and feared; and it was to prevent that, that I wanted to kill myself.

HELMER. I would gladly work night and day for you, Nora— 345 bear sorrow and want for your sake. But no man would sacrifice his honour for the one he loves.

NORA. It is a thing hundreds of thousands of women have done.

HELMER. Oh, you think and talk like a heedless child.

NORA. Maybe. But you neither think nor talk like the man I could bind myself to. As soon as your fear was over—and it was not fear for what threatened me, but for what might happen to you— when the whole thing was past, as far as you were concerned it was exactly as if nothing at all had happened. Exactly as before, I was your little skylark, your doll, which you would in future treat with doubly gentle care, because it was so brittle and fragile. [*getting up*] Torvald— it was then it dawned upon me that for eight years I had been living here with a strange man, and had borne him three children—. Oh, I can't bear to think of it! I could tear myself into little bits!

HELMER. [*sadly*] I see, I see. An Abyss has opened between us— there is no denying it. But, Nora, would it not be possible to fill it up?

NORA.   As I am now, I am no wife for you.   350

HELMER.   I have it in me to become a different man.

NORA.   Perhaps—if your doll is taken away from you.

HELMER.   But to part!—to part from you! No, no, Nora, I can't understand that idea.

NORA.   [*going out to the right*] That makes it all the more certain that it must be done.

[*She comes back with her cloak and hat and a small bag which she puts on a chair by the table.*]

HELMER.   Nora, Nora, not now! Wait till to-morrow.   355

NORA.   [*putting on her cloak*] I cannot spend the night in a strange man's room.

HELMER.   But can't we live here like brother and sister—?

NORA.   [*putting on her hat*] You know very well that would not last long. [*puts the shawl round her*] Good-bye, Torvald. I won't see the little ones. I know they are in better hands than mine. As I am now, I can be of no use to them.

HELMER.   But some day, Nora—some day?

NORA.   How can I tell? I have no idea what is going to become   360
of me.

HELMER.   But you are my wife, whatever becomes of you.

NORA.   Listen, Torvald. I have heard that when a wife deserts her husband's house, as I am doing now, he is legally freed from all obligations towards her. In any case I set you free from all your obligations. You are not to feel yourself bound in the slightest way, any more than I shall. There must be perfect freedom on both sides. See here is your ring back. Give me mine.

HELMER.   That too?

NORA.   That too.

HELMER.   Here it is.   365

NORA.   That's right. Now it is all over. I have put the keys here. The maids know all about everything in the house—better than I do. To-morrow, after I have left her, Christine will come here and pack up my own things that I brought with me from home. I will have them sent after me.

HELMER.   All over! All over!—Nora, shall you never think of me again?

NORA.   I know I shall often think of you and the children and this house.

HELMER.   May I write to you, Nora?

NORA.   No—never. You must not do that.   370
HELMER.   But at least let me send you—
NORA.   Nothing—nothing—
HELMER.   Let me help you if you are in want.
NORA.   No. I can receive nothing from a stranger.
HELMER.   Nora—can I never be anything more than a stranger   375
to you?
NORA.   [*taking her bag*] Ah, Torvald, the most wonderful thing of
all would have to happen.
HELMER.   Tell me what that would be!
NORA.   Both you and I would have to be so changed that—. Oh,
Torvald, I don't believe any longer in wonderful things happening.
HELMER.   But I will believe in it. Tell me? So changed that—?
NORA.   That our life together would be a real wedlock.   380
Good-bye.

[She goes out through the hall.]

HELMER.   [*sinks down on a chair at the door and buries his face in his
hands*] Nora! Nora! [*looks round, and rises*] Empty. She is gone. [*A hope
flashes across his mind.*] The most wonderful thing of all—?

[The sound of a door slamming is heard from below.]

Acknowledgments

Auden, W. H. "Musee des Beaux Arts," copyright 1940 and renewed 1968 by W. H. Auden, from *Collected Poems* by W. H. Auden. Used by permission of Random House, Inc.

Brooks, Gwendolyn. "We Real Cool" by Gwendolyn Brooks from *Blacks*. Reprinted by Consent of Brooks Permissions.

De Maupassant, Guy. "The Necklace" by Guy de Maupassant in *Literature: An Introduction to Reading and Writing, 7/E*, by Edgar V. Roberts/Henry E. Jacobs, 2004, ©. Reprinted by permission of Pearson Education, Inc., Upper Saddle River, NJ.

Faulkner, William. "A Rose for Emily," copyright 1930 and renewed 1958 by William Faulkner, from *Collected Stories of William Faulkner* by William Faulkner. Used by permission of Random House, Inc.

Frost, Robert. "Mending Wall" from *The Poetry of Robert Frost* edited by Edward Connery Lathem. Copyright Lesley Frost Ballantine 1964, 1967, copyright 1936, 1958 by Robert Frost, copyright 1930, © 1969 by Henry Holt and Company. Reprinted by permission of Henry Holt and Company, LLC.

Frost, Robert. "Design" from *The Poetry of Robert Frost* edited by Edward Connery Lathem. Copyright Lesley Frost Ballantine 1964, 1967, copyright 1936, 1958 by Robert Frost, copyright 1930 © 1969 by Henry Holt and Company. Reprinted by permission of Henry Holt and Company, LLC.

Hayden Robert. "The Winter Sundays." Copyright © 1966 by Robert Hayden, from *Collected Poems of Robert Hayden* by Robert Hayden, edited by Frederick Glaysher. Used by permission of Liveright Publishing Corporation.

Yeats, W. B. "Leda and the Swan" is reprinted with the permission of Scribner, an imprint of Simon & Schuster Adult Publishing Group, from *The Collected Works of W. B. Yeats, Volume I: The Poems, Revised,* edited by Richard J. Finneran. Copyright © 1928 by The Macmillan Company; copyright renewed © 1956 by Georgie Yeats. Reprinted with permission of A. P. Watt Ltd. on behalf of Michael B. Yeats.